Shire County Guide 7

SHROPSHIRE

Lawrence Garner

Shire Publications Ltd

2

Printed in Great Britain by CIT Printing Services, Press Buildings, Merlins Bridge, Haverfordwest, Dyfed SA61 1XF.

British Library Cataloguing in Publication Data:
Garner, Lawrence
Shropshire. — 3Rev. ed. — (Shire County Guides; No. 7)
I. Title II. Series
914.24504
ISBN 0-7478-0202-5

Acknowledgements

The publishers acknowledge the assistance of James Dyer and Dr Barrie Trinder in the preparation of this book. The map of Shropshire on pages 4 and 5 was drawn by Robert Dizon and the plan of Shrewsbury on page 28 is by D. R. Darton. All photographs are by the author, except the cover photograph and those on pages 13, 20, 22, 29, 33, 34, 37, 48, 65, 66, 70, 71, 74, 76, 77, 78, 79, 81, 82, 84, 85 and 90, which are by Cadbury Lamb.

Ordnance Survey grid references

Although information on how to reach most of the places described in this book by car is given in the text, National Grid References are also included in many instances, particularly for the harder-to-find places in chapters 3, 4 and 7, for the benefit of those readers who have the Ordnance Survey 1:50,000 Landranger maps of the area. The references are stated as a Landranger sheet number followed by the 100 km National Grid square and the six-figure reference.

To locate a site by means of the grid reference, proceed as in the following example: The Berth (OS 126: SJ 429236). Take the OS Landranger map sheet 126 ('Shrewsbury & surrounding area'). The grid numbers are printed in blue around the edges of the map. (In more recently produced maps these numbers are repeated at 10 km intervals throughout the map, so that it is not necessary to open it out completely.) Read off these numbers from the left along the top edge of the map until you come to 42, denoting a vertical grid line, then estimate nine-tenths of the distance to vertical line 43 and envisage an imaginary vertical grid line 42.9 at this point. Next look at the grid numbers at one side of the map (either side will do) and read upwards until you find the horizontal grid line 23. Estimate six-tenths of the distance to the next horizontal line above (i.e. 24), and so envisage an imaginary horizontal line across the map at 23.6. Follow this imaginary line across the map until it crosses the imaginary vertical line 42.9. At the intersection of these two lines you will find The Berth.

The Ordnance Survey Landranger maps which cover Shropshire are sheets 126, 127, 137 and 138. Very small areas of the county are found on maps 117, 118 and 136.

Cover: *A view towards Ludlow.*

Contents

PLACES TO VISIT IN SHROPSHIRE

- ■ Town or village (chapter 2)
- 🖪 Town or village with information centre (chapters 2 and 11)
- ⅍ Country parks, nature reserves, etc. (chapter 3)
- ⊓ Archaeological sites (chapter 4)
- ♟ Castles (chapter 5)
- ‡ Monastic buildings (chapter 5)
- † Churches (chapter 6)
- ⊞ Houses and gardens (chapter 7)
- 🏛 Museums (chapter 8)
- ⌁ Industrial history sites (chapter 9)
- ● Other places
- ══ Principal road

0   5   10   15 kilometres
0   5   10 miles

Llangollen
Overton
Chirk
CLWYD
The Mere
Selattyn † Wat's ELLESMERE 🖪⅍
Dyke Welsh Frankton
Cefn Coch ⅍ Whittington ⅍ Colem
Old Oswestry
Oswestry Old ⅍ 🖪 OSWESTRY Lockgate Bridge
Racecourse 🏛 Rednal
Queen's Head Westonwharf
Maesbury Marsh West Felton
Llanyblodwel ■ † ⅍ Pant Woolston ⊓ The
Llanymynech Hills Knockin ■ Ruyton Berth
-Xl-Towns Baschurc
Llanymynech Nesscliffe ■ ⊞ Adcote
Melverley ⅍
†
Alberbury
A458
Lyth
Pontesbury Hill
Minsterley ⅍ Earl
WELSHPOOL Poles Coppice ⅍ Hill
⌁ Snailbeach
Llanfair A458
Caereinion Chirbury Stiperstones
† ⅍ Cardi
Mitchell's ⅍ Mill Val.
POWYS Fold Bog Mine
Montgomery Rectory Wood ⅍
A489 Church
Caersws NEWTOWN Little Stretton † Stretton
Bishop's Acton Scott 🏛
Castle
LLANIDLOES Colstey Bank ⅍
Bettws-y Bury Ditches ⊓ Hopesay Hill Nor
-crwyn ⅍ Ca
† Craven Arms ■ ⊓
Clun Stokesay ♟🏛
Wernlas Collection
Caer
⊓ Caradoc
KNIGHTON Leintwardine
A4113

N

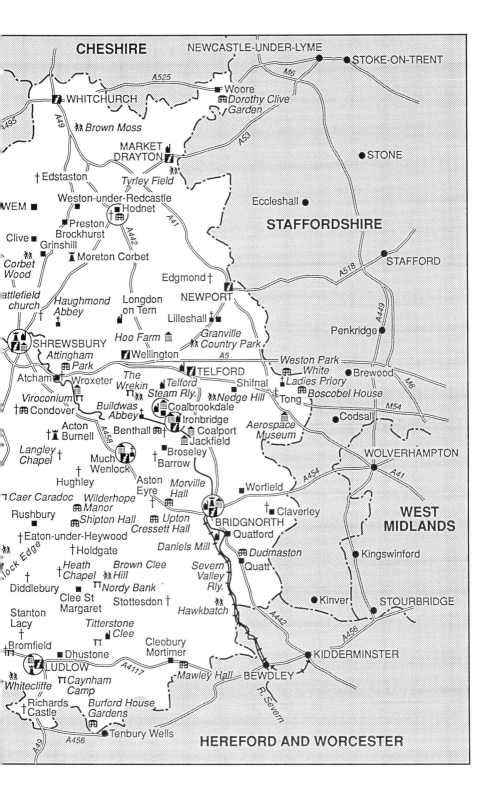

Preface

Welcome to the Shire County Guide to Shropshire, one of over thirty such books, written and designed to enable you to organise your time in the county well.

The Shire County Guides fill the need for a compact, accurate and thorough guide to each county so that visitors can plan a half-day excursion or a whole week's stay to best advantage. Residents, too, will find the guides a handy and reliable reference to the places of interest in their area.

Travelling British roads can be time consuming, and the County Guides will ensure that you need not inadvertently miss any interesting feature in a locality, that you do not accidentally bypass a new museum or an outstanding church, that you can find an attractive place to picnic, and that you will appreciate the history and the buildings of the towns or villages in which you stop.

This book has been arranged in special interest chapters, such as the countryside, historic houses or archaeological sites, and all these places of interest are located on the map on pages 4-5. Use the map either for an overview to decide which area has most to interest you, or to help you enjoy your immediate neighbourhood. Then refer to the nearest town or village in chapter 2 to see, at a glance, what special features or attractions each community contains or is near. The subsequent chapters enable readers with a particular interest to find immediately those places of importance to them, while the cross-referencing under 'Shropshire towns and villages' assists readers with wider tastes to select how best to spend their time.

1
A view of Shropshire

Shropshire first achieved an identity early in the tenth century, when the area known as *Scrobbescire*, governed from its principal settlement *Scrobbesbyrig*, was delineated, possibly as a way of organising defence against the Danes. However, the acquisition of a name and a boundary was only one stage in the history of a border district that had been of strategic importance for a long time.

We know almost nothing about the earliest inhabitants of Shropshire. The hostile terrain of marshland and bleak hills did not attract prehistoric settlers in large numbers, although a few implements of the mesolithic and neolithic ages have been found in the southern part of the county. The first substantial evidence of prehistoric life relates to the bronze age. A stone circle at Mitchell's Fold, near Chirbury, can still be seen and a cemetery has been excavated at Bromfield, but the most important signs of prehistoric activity are two tracks: the Port Way over the Long Mynd, and the Clee-Clun Ridgeway running across south Shropshire from the Kerry Hills, south of Newtown in Powys, to the river Severn at what is now Bewdley.

The iron age brought the first systematic settlement in the north. In the seventh century BC a Celtic people colonised the Severn valley around a natural 'capital' on the Wrekin, and in the process they established the hillforts which are such a feature of the county. About 25 major hill sites have been identified, and they were not just military outposts but important communities. Some of the lowland farms along the Severn have also been traced, particularly in the Shrewsbury area.

By the time the Romans reached this part of England in about AD 50 it is likely that these settlers, whom the Romans called Cornovii, controlled much of what is now Shropshire. How the Romans subdued them is not clear. The campaign involved a legendary last stand by the British chieftain Caractacus (or Caradoc) at a place which has not yet been identified, and the Roman army was able to establish a large camp in about AD 58 at Wroxeter, close to the Wrekin, in order to further their campaign against the Welsh.

Wroxeter (*Viroconium*) served as an army base for thirty years before Chester was chosen as a better strategic position, and *Viroconium* was handed over to the Cornovii as a town planned and built by Roman engineers. A similar process occurred further north, where a military camp developed into the town of *Mediolanum*, on a site now occupied by Whitchurch. There is evidence too that the Romans exploited the lead deposits near the Stiperstones and mined for copper at Llanymynech to the south-west of Oswestry. By this time Watling Street (approximately the route of the present A5) was well established as an important road, and another major Roman road ran from *Mediolanum* to *Bravonium* (Leintwardine, west of Ludlow).

The Cornovii seem to have survived for a long time after the departure of the Romans, although not with their former supremacy. The border country was thrown into a confused sequence of power struggles, civil wars and Saxon maraudings, but for nearly two hundred years of the post-Roman period the principal rulers of the future Shropshire were Celtic chieftains. English dominance increased during the seventh century, particularly under Penda of Mercia, who killed his rival Oswald of Northumbria at the battle of Oswestry in 642, and about twenty years later Mercian rule was formally confirmed by a treaty with the Welsh.

The Mercian kings left their mark on Shropshire. They built Wat's Dyke, an earthwork stretching from the Dee estuary to a point south of Oswestry. Its purpose remains obscure, and it tends to be overshadowed by King Offa's great dyke constructed along the entire length of the Welsh border in the late eighth century.

The next threat to Mercia was to come not from the Welsh but from the Danes, who first gained a substantial foothold in eastern England in 865. Ten years later they were able to set up a puppet king of Mercia, who proved to be the last of the line. Although the Danes established at least one outpost in Shropshire at Quatford, the county never suffered long-term occupation, and local opposition to the Scandinavian invaders was organised successfully by Aethelflaed, daughter of Alfred the Great.

Defence against the Normans proved less easy. Edric the Wild, a local resistance hero who became a legendary figure, led an unsuccessful attack on the Norman garrison at Shrewsbury in 1069, but the only result was a scourging of the county and the arrival of Roger de Montgomery as Earl of Shrewsbury. He and his two successors reigned as virtually independent rulers for the next thirty years, building formidable castles at Shrewsbury, Bridgnorth and Montgomery. Lesser baronial families like the Fitzalans, the Corbets, the Fitzwarines and the Le Stranges controlled smaller areas from their own castles.

For four hundred years these 'Marcher Lords' dominated Shropshire. They derived their power from the king's need for strong forces along the Welsh border and they took full advantage of their extraordinary autonomy. Sometimes allies, often enemies, they fought the Welsh and they fought each other, imposing an arbitrary and unpredictable regime on the people under their control, who could rarely rely on royal law for protection.

Before the final pacification of the mid seventeenth century the county suffered not only innumerable local conflicts but also major wars including the battles of King John and Henry III with Llywelyn the Great between 1211 and 1234, the revolt of Simon de Montfort, the Welsh campaigns of Edward I, the revolt of Owain Glyndwr and the Earl of Northumberland, the Wars of the Roses and finally the Civil War, when at least a dozen sieges took place in the county.

Since then Shropshire has enjoyed a period of tranquillity, encouraged by the existence of an unusually large number of landed estates. The majority have been owned by families content to farm their acres and preserve the *status quo*. But while most of the county concerned itself with agriculture, a dramatic revolution of a beneficial kind took place in the area now occupied by the new town of Telford. The remarkable discoveries and technological developments that took

Clun Forest, viewed from Bettws-y-crwyn church.

A section of the ramparts of Old Oswestry hillfort.

place in and around the Severn Gorge in the eighteenth and early nineteenth centuries are outlined in chapter 8 (Ironbridge Gorge Museum), but this area of Shropshire can justifiably claim to have changed the course of civilisation.

The period since the 1830s has been a time of economic regression for the county. Heavy industry has all but disappeared, mining has ceased, the former big quarrying enterprises have contracted, most of the railways have gone, and the bright dream of a thriving new town has been dispelled by unfavourable national circumstances. It might have been disastrous, yet life goes on cheerfully enough. Shropshire farmers are among the most efficient in Britain, and elsewhere livings are earned in a wide variety of small but resilient enterprises.

Tourism has become increasingly important to the county in recent years, although the policy has been to avoid the aggressive marketing of its many attractions. The appeal of Shropshire to the discerning visitor lies in an unspoilt landscape of unexpected variety. Indeed it contains a complete cross-section of English inland landscape with some unusual features.

In the extreme north-west Shropshire merges imperceptibly with the uplands of mid Wales. It is an area where small hills crowd together, hiding an intricate system of valleys. Sheep and dairy farming exist on equal terms, managed from small family farms and relying largely on pastureland.

East of Oswestry there is an abrupt transition to the huge plain that extends well into Cheshire — rich dairy and arable country with red buildings made from the underlying sandstone, which occasionally relieves the flatness with sudden ridges and outcrops. Here too glacial debris, recent in geological terms, has produced an area of 'meres and mosses', lakes and fens of great interest to naturalists. The plain continues to the Staffordshire border, providing on the eastern side a type of landscape that is more typically English, with big arable farms, larger villages and some commuter settlement dependent on Wolverhampton and the Potteries.

Further south, the central belt of the county is dominated by two towns. Shrewsbury lies close to the centre of Shropshire, as befits the county town; it sprawls now well beyond its original nucleus and acts as a natural centre for a widespread rural area. To the east,

Telford is being created on the site of the old Shropshire coalfield, which had become a wasteland when industry petered out. There is a vast amount of new building here among the reclaimed spoil tips, but Telford also takes in some well established older settlements like Wellington, Oakengates and Dawley. At its southern end the new town includes Ironbridge and Coalbrookdale, proclaimed as 'the birthplace of industry' and now being conserved as a living memory to pioneering technology.

To the south of Shrewsbury lies a remarkable series of hill ranges. On the map they can be seen as four parallel lines, each of a different character, running from north-east to south-west. Wenlock Edge, a dramatic escarpment 15 miles (24 km) long, is the most easterly and presents a formidable obstacle to communications. The Stretton Hills, dominated by the whale-backed Lawley and the sharp peak of Caer Caradoc, confront the high plateaux of the Long Mynd range on the other side of the Church Stretton valley. Finally there is the strange series of outcrops known as the Stiperstones, lying close to former lead mines.

It is an area of great geological interest. Wenlock Edge is mainly limestone, the Stretton Hills are composed of volcanic debris, the Stiperstones are quartzite, while the Long Mynd contains a variety of rock, much of it pre-Cambrian and among the oldest in Britain. The Church Stretton Fault is a famous geological feature, making the district a potential earthquake area. It is fine walking country.

The extreme south-west of the county is different again. Here the Clun Forest merges with the moorlands of Kerry and Radnor over the border, and the prevailing landscape is sharply undulating heathland and sheep pasture, occasionally rising to a height of 1500 feet (450 metres). It is sparsely populated, and villages are small and few in number.

Finally there is the area to the south-east, lying behind Wenlock Edge and overshadowed by Shropshire's highest hills, Brown Clee and Titterstone Clee. In some ways this seems an alien district, possibly because the natural lines of communication pass it by on each side through Bridgnorth and Ludlow. It has more affinity with the neighbouring county of Hereford and Worcester, with the Wyre Forest lying across the county boundary. This is sandstone country again, although the extensive quarrying of the two peaks has been aimed at extracting the hard basalt capping, which is used for road construction.

One characteristic of the county is the lack of what most people think of as villages — sizable settlements with a range of housing, a church, a school, a pub and a shop or two. Apart from Shrewsbury and Telford, the towns tend to be small, intimate communities providing services for the surrounding rural area. Outside the towns the predominant form of settlement is the hamlet.

There are various reasons for this. One is that Shropshire (apart from its eastern fringes) is not under pressure from commuters, whose housing demands have forced the growth of villages in other Midland counties like Warwickshire. (It remains to be seen whether the recent development of fast road links to the north-west will attract a 'commuter invasion' from the Liverpool conurbation.) Another more basic reason is the fact that many medieval settlements that might have been expected to develop in size withered instead. They were formed as farming communities in the middle of open fields and common land but disintegrated when enclosures encouraged the establishment of isolated farmsteads in their own fields. Also, many of Shropshire's medieval hamlets developed around castles or monastic buildings that afterwards ceased to function. Finally, in more recent times, the rapid rise and decline of industries such as lead mining in the Snailbeach area or quarrying in the Clee Hills have led to settlements being quickly formed and then stranded without further purpose.

The combination of small compact towns and modest hamlets makes Shropshire a genuinely rural county, comparatively unknown and open to exploration.

2
Shropshire
towns and villages

It is not always easy to make a clear-cut distinction between towns and villages in Shropshire. Places like Craven Arms or Clun undoubtedly have the feel of towns, but in other counties they would rate as villages in terms of population, size or facilities. The characteristic form of settlement in Shropshire is the hamlet and the 'typical' village is rare. This chapter describes the towns of Shropshire and villages and hamlets that have either an exceptional collection of buildings or a highly individual character. Other villages that have specific attractions are listed here with cross-references to guide the reader to descriptions of those features in other chapters.

Acton Burnell

Castle, page 51; church of St Mary, page 58; Langley Chapel, page 63.

Acton Scott

Historic Working Farm, page 78.

Alberbury

Despite a scattering of modern houses it is still possible to find the ancient nucleus of Alberbury, just off the B4393 10 miles (16 km) west of Shrewsbury. In the Norman and early medieval period it was a border settlement of some importance, with a castle, a church and a priory. Little has been done to preserve the ruins of the castle, built by Fulke Fitzwarine in the early thirteenth century, and they are now in a dangerous condition, although part of the keep can be studied from the road.

Nowadays the dominant building is the church of St Michael and All Angels, standing on a rise in the old village centre, with a fortress-like tower topped by a saddleback roof. It is remarkably big for a village church, and uncomfortably dark because of a decision in the 1840s to rebuild the chancel in Norman style with windows of minimal size. The nave roof is magnificent, incorporating semi-circular arched braces and five rows of wind braces, but the centre of interest is the fourteenth-century south chapel, which was later given over to monuments of the Leighton family, who have lived at nearby Loton Park for over three hundred years. A member of the family was responsible for the attractive Art Nouveau window in the south wall.

From the main road Loton Park is visible across the fields, a mixture of Jacobean, early Georgian and Victorian styles. The area to the south of the road is well-known to sports-car enthusiasts as a hill-climb venue.

Aston Eyre

Church, page 58.

Atcham

Apart from the church there is much to interest visitors in this little riverside settlement 4 miles (6.5 km) south-east of Shrewsbury. The principal building is the Mytton and Mermaid Hotel, a splendid late Georgian house with an elegant stable block. Next to the filling station is a thatched *cottage ornée* — actually a semi-detached pair — that was no doubt the fanciful whim of the owner of nearby Attingham Park. It stands close to an L-shaped group of Gothick estate cottages, and this architectural theme is repeated in gate lodges a short distance up the Upton Magna road opposite. There are two bridges across the river here. The redundant one was the work of John Gwynne. Built in 1771, it carried Thomas Telford's original Holyhead Road, and a walk across it will reveal one of Telford's distinctive milestones.

Church of St Eata, page 58; **Attingham Park** historic house, page 67.

In the locality: Viroconium Roman City and Museum, page 49.

Barrow

Church of St Giles, page 58.

Baschurch

Midway between Oswestry and Shrewsbury on the B4397, the original hamlet of Baschurch underwent a Victorian expansion with the arrival of the Shrewsbury-Chester railway, and in recent years it has attracted much modern housing, but its village character still survives around the church. Built of local red sandstone, All Saints takes its character largely from restorations in the 1790s (by Telford) and 1890s. Nearby are a substantial timber-framed house and several interesting cottages of various ages.

The Berth prehistoric earthwork, page 46.

In the locality: Adcote historic house, page 67; Westonwharf, page 88.

Benthall

Church of St Bartholomew, page 59; Benthall Hall, page 67.

Bettws-y-crwyn

Church of St Mary, page 59.

Bishop's Castle

Market day, Friday.

Until 1832 Bishop's Castle returned two members to Parliament, and until 1967 it was England's smallest borough. Now deprived of these distinctions, it remains a friendly rural centre with an unhurried pace of life. The main street is on a steep slope, and originally the castle stood at the top of the hill and the church at the bottom; the remains of the castle are now negligible, but the church is still there, a stolid Victorian rebuild on a spacious scale with a striking arrangement of roof timbers over the chancel and an interesting seventeenth-century bust of George Needham in the south transept. Near its gates is a cluster of attractive buildings of various periods, including a handsome Georgian house in mellow brick and an unusual timber-framed cottage with dormer windows. Fur-ther up the street a similar blend of architecture is revealed, and a number of immaculately maintained old pubs are a reminder that this is still a market town.

The High Street narrows sharply at the top, where the miniature eighteenth-century town hall almost closes it off. The borough jail once occupied its ground floor. Next to it is the 'house on crutches', an Elizabethan dwelling with its gable end supported on wooden posts. Dominating the small market square beyond is the imposing Castle Hotel, and the small shops and houses in the square and in Bull Street beyond make this a picturesque spot. Salop Street leads off to the right and contains a shrine of real ale enthusiasts — the Three Tuns, a pub with an unpretentious frontage but with its own brewery next door.

In the locality: Offa's Dyke, pages 38 and 49; Bury Ditches iron age fort, page 46; Colstey Bank picnic site, page 40; The Stiperstones, page 42.

Bouldon

Heath Chapel, page 61.

Bridgnorth

Early closing, Thursday; market days, Monday and Saturday.

Bridgnorth is a divided town. Set on and below a massive sandstone bluff beside the Severn, High Town and Low Town are connected by one motor road, many flights of steps and a cliff railway. Until the mid nineteenth century Bridgnorth was a thriving river port, and in earlier years it was an important iron-producing town and had several carpet mills. Today it is a fascinating place for visitors, with its centre still unspoilt and its extensive new housing unobtrusively tucked away.

On the west side of the bridge it is still possible to see the wharves and port buildings. The sandstone cliffs rise behind them, dotted with caves that were once used as houses and storage places. The precipitous Cartway, once the only way up for vehicles, rises from here, with the well-preserved house of Bishop Percy at the bottom and the handsome Prince Charles inn nearby. On turning left at the top of the Cartway, you pass the extraordinary Victorian market hall, built in

St Mary's church and the bridge at Bridgnorth.

an incongruous Italian style, and enter East Castle Street, Bridgnorth's most elegant thoroughfare. The fine Georgian houses lead the eye to Thomas Telford's church of St Mary, a light and spacious building of classical proportions. Behind the church is a small park on the site of the former castle, of which only a portion of the keep remains, leaning at an almost impossible angle. From the ramparts here there is a good view of the station area, now the northern terminus of the Severn Valley Railway.

Back in the High Street, the most noticeable building is the Town Hall, a timber-framed structure erected in 1652 and still straddling the road. Several more timber-framed buildings stand nearby, with the Swan inn especially prominent, and the whole wide street is a harmonious mixture of architectural styles, closed off by the Northgate, rebuilt in 1910. Just before Northgate, Church Street leads off to the right. It has some interesting almshouses and brings you into the 'close' surrounding St Leonard's church.

In this tranquil area stands the cottage occupied by the puritan preacher Richard Baxter in 1640 (see page 93), together with another curious group of almshouses and the original grammar school. It is possible to descend St Leonard's Steps from here, rejoining the Cartway and arriving back at the bridge.

There is little of interest on the other side of the river, but at the eastern end of the bridge is a tower commemorating the work of Richard Trevithick and J. U. Raistrick, who built the first steam passenger locomotive at John Hazeldine's ironworks here in 1808. The bridge provides a final panorama of what is the most striking of the Severnside towns.

Castle, page 51; **Bridgnorth Museum**, page 78; **Costume and Childhood Museum**, page 78; **Midland Motor Museum**, page 79; **Severn Valley Railway**, page 87; **Daniels Mill**, page 85; **Cliff Railway**, page 85.

In the locality: churches at Aston Eyre, page 58, and Claverley, page 60; Dudmaston Hall, page 74; Morville Hall, page 75; Upton Cressett Hall, page 75.

Bromfield

Church of St Mary, page 59; bronze age cemetery, page 46.

Broseley

Until its decline in the later nineteenth century Broseley, situated on the river opposite Ironbridge, was an important centre of industry in the Severn Gorge. It produced coal and bricks but was perhaps best known as the headquarters of the ironmaster John Wilkinson. Later the town fell into decay, but the development of the new town of Telford across the river led to its revival. Properties with character were bought up and restored, and Broseley regained its bustling life. It is not a pretty place, but the architectural enthusiast will find a wealth of domestic building styles of the eighteenth and nineteenth centuries in the course of a walk along its main street, starting at the impressive Victorian church. Directly opposite is The Lawns, John Wilkinson's home for a short time, and a little further on is a twin-gabled house of 1663 — a Stuart manor marooned in an urban setting. The High Street has a few original buildings, and it is worth wandering down the side streets, which still reveal the haphazard development of an early Victorian industrial settlement. This impression is reinforced at the top of the main street, where the view opens out to show houses of various ages scattered in the fields around the town.

In the locality: Barrow church, page 58; Benthall church and Hall, pages 59 and 67; Ironbridge Gorge Museum, page 81; Underwater World, page 84.

Buildwas

Buildwas Abbey, page 56.

Burford

Burford House Gardens and Treasures Plant Centre, page 71.

Caynham

Caynham Camp iron age enclosure, page 47.

Chirbury

Mitchells Fold stone circle, page 47; Offa's Dyke, pages 38 and 49; church of St Michael, page 59.

Church Stretton

Early closing, Wednesday; market day, Thursday.

Church Stretton never succeeded in becoming a fashionable spa but it enjoyed much popularity as a late Victorian health resort, and it still retains something of that atmosphere. It is the 'capital' of the Long Mynd, the largest of a string of settlements along the foot of the hills, and has a fine setting with views across the valley to Caer Caradoc and the Lawley. Information about the surrounding hills is available at the Information Centre, and the town is a natural starting point for walks into the hills.

Church Stretton is of minor interest in itself but pleasant to walk round. From the car park you emerge into Sandford Avenue, one of the main shopping streets. It was developed in the late nineteenth century, and to reach the older part of the town you need to walk up to the little square. There are some attractive small buildings here, including a fine traditional ironmonger's shop, and more to be seen in the road leading out of the square to the south. A turning off this road climbs to the Long Mynd Hotel, which occupies a commanding position above the town; it was originally designed as the spa hydro and is the only substantial survival of the old spa buildings.

Also accessible from the square is St Laurence's church. Although not distinguished architecturally, it has one surprising feature: a Sheila-na-gig over a disused north door. This is a female fertility figure of a rather gross kind, one of four in Shropshire. Inside the church there is a striking modern memorial in the transept roof.

In the locality: Rectory Wood, page 40; Edge Wood, page 39; Carding Mill Valley, page 42; the Long Mynd, page 42; Caer Caradoc iron age fort, page 46; churches at Eaton-under-Heywood, page 61, and Little Stretton, page 63; Wilderhope Manor, page 75; Acton Scott Historic Working Farm, page 78.

Claverley

Set in a very rural situation 6 miles (10 km) east of Bridgnorth, Claverley is one of Shropshire's few conventional villages and is extremely attractive. The centrepiece, apart from the church, is the former rectory, an impressive timber-framed house outside the church gates, with the handsome Old School House next door. The short, steep village street is lined with a pleasant mixture of old shops and houses. Two of the village's three pubs, the King's Arms and the Crown, stand together, trying to outdo one another in quaintness, while the Plough remains aloof at the top. With its odd nooks and crannies, Claverley is a village that repays a leisurely walk.

Church of All Saints, page 60.

Clee St Margaret

In an area close to the Clee Hills and noted more for its functional industrial settlements, it is strange to come across Clee St Margaret, probably the nearest Shropshire has to a 'picturesque village'. Many of the old small cottages have been converted and 'gentrified', but the unique feature is the fact that the Clee Brook runs along one of the main village roads, forming what may well be the longest ford in Britain.

In the locality: Brown Clee Hill, page 38; Nordy Bank iron age fort, page 47; Heath Chapel, page 61.

Cleobury Mortimer

Market day, alternate Wednesdays.
Approached from the Clee Hills, the town is immediately recognisable by the crooked church spire. 'Town' is something of a courtesy title, but Cleobury Mortimer is the natural centre for the scattered hamlets of this thinly populated area. The most notable buildings line the single main street, which slopes and curves gracefully, offering much to interest students of domestic architecture.

The top end of the street is dominated by a magnificent house in Queen Anne style, with a well-restored cottage opposite. Old-fashioned shop fronts form harmonious terraces on each side of the road, but the line is broken in startling fashion on the right by Beaconsfield, a house in classic Regency style that would not look out of place in Bath. Equally handsome is the Vicarage, a little further down — stone-faced and beautifully proportioned, with a sag that suggests timber-framing behind the façade.

The High Street, Cleobury Mortimer.

St Mary's church is lofty and spacious, although the south arcade and wall lean alarmingly as a result of pressure from the roof. Thomas Telford made one attempt at strapping it and Sir Giles Gilbert Scott took similar precautions at the 1872 restoration. Possibly the same structural problem has caused the chancel arch and the Norman west arch to assume a horseshoe shape. The fine east window of 1875 is unique in being a memorial to William Langland, the fourteenth-century author of *Piers Plowman*.

At the lower end of the street the King's Arms is notable, but perhaps the best of the town's smaller buildings are in the Georgian terrace opposite the post office; they are of varying shapes and sizes, and one has elegant semicircular bow windows.

In the locality: Titterstone Clee Hill, pages 49 and 88; Stottesdon church, page 66; Mawley Hall, page 74.

Clive

See under Grinshill, page 18.

Clun church.

ing and a dignified wooded reredos. The canopied pulpit is Jacobean. A vestry was turned into an impressive Lady Chapel, and next to the door from here into the chancel is a wooden panel marked out by the carver but only partly completed. An interesting feature at the back of the church is a painting of St George by an Abyssinian artist, presented in memory of a local man killed during the Second World War.

The castle is reached by crossing the bridge and passing through a gate on the left just after it. The site is notable not so much for the ruins as for the surrounding earthworks, which have been turned into a pleasant park. There are no outstanding buildings in the streets of the town, where a charming muddle of houses and shops on a small scale produces a very intimate atmosphere. However, the Holy Trinity Hospital, an attractive block of almshouses of 1618 with their own chapel, should not be missed.

Castle, page 51; **Local History Museum**, page 79.

In the locality: Offa's Dyke, pages 38 and 49; Bury Ditches, page 46; Caer Caradoc hillfort, page 47; Bettws-y-crwyn church, page 59.

Clun

Market day, Tuesday.

Set in the centre of the Clun Forest, the town is a solitary but cheerful place where there always seems to be a great deal going on. Clun consists of two distinct parts. The 'old' town, grouped round the Norman church at the top of the hill, gave place to a new planned community on the other side of the river when the castle was built. The bridge between them is a fine example of a packhorse bridge with pedestrian alcoves.

The squat and massive tower of St George's church looks primitive and could have been built originally with defence in mind, but the church interior is very sophisticated as a result of restoration by G. E. Street, one of the great Victorian church specialists. In the nave he was content to reveal the fine roof timbers and repair the Norman columns, but the chancel was completely remodelled with the addition of a heavy screen, elaborate wood carv-

Coalbrookdale

The name of Coalbrookdale has always had a place in the history books as the site of the furnace where Abraham Darby transformed the production of cast iron. The unearthing of Darby's original furnace in 1959 was the starting point of Britain's most ambitious programme of industrial conservation, resulting in the Ironbridge Gorge Museum (see chapter 8) and the preservation of much of the gorge's distinctive architectural heritage.

The settlement is reached by a lane off the riverside road on the western outskirts of Ironbridge. It climbs steadily, passing the rather gaunt Victorian parish church, to reach the Great Warehouse of 1838, which now houses the Museum of Iron and Darby's furnace. It is possible to park here and walk around the area (a useful booklet is available at the museum). Among the features of interest are the surviving water-supply arrangements to the furnace, the 'gentry houses' in Darby Road, including Rosehill House, now open to the public, three terraces of early workers' cottages, a former school and a corn mill. The most striking feature of Coalbrookdale is its compactness, with workers' accommodation and owners' houses alike huddled around the furnace site.

Ironbridge Gorge Museum (Elton Gallery, Museum of Iron and Furnace, Rosehill House), page 18; industrial history, page 85.

In the locality: Buildwas Abbey, page 56; Telford Steam Railway, page 88.

Coalport

Tar Tunnel, page 82; China Museum, page 82.

Condover

Lyth Hill, page 40; church of St Mary and St Andrew, page 60; Condover Hall, page 71.

Cosford

Aerospace Museum, page 79.

Craven Arms

Although it makes no claims to beauty, Craven Arms is unique in Shropshire as the only town to have been created entirely as a result of railway development. It takes its name from the inn that still stands at a junction of roads that were important sheep-droving routes from mid Wales to the English markets. After the Shrewsbury-Hereford railway was laid, a junction for Central Wales was built here, and later two other branch lines were constructed a little to the north. A planned new town was established with the aim of providing services for the large catchment area created by the railway links. The town became important as a place where huge numbers of sheep were sold and dispatched all over Britain. The sales still take place, though lorries have replaced the special trains. Craven Arms is devoted to commercial activity and retains the rather impermanent air of a prairie town.

In the locality: Edge Wood, page 39; Hopesay Hill, page 42; Wenlock Edge, page 43; Norton Camp, page 47; Stokesay Castle, page 53; churches at Diddlebury, page 61, and Stokesay, page 64; Acton Scott Historic Working Farm, page 78; the Wernlas Collection, Onibury, page 83.

Dhustone

(OS 137: SO 587763)

About 5 miles (8 km) east of Ludlow, and lying north of the A4117 at OS 137: SO 587763, Dhustone is an example of a once active quarrying community that has become almost a ghost village. One or two haphazard terraces still stand in their exposed situation halfway up Titterstone Clee, but not many of the houses appear to be occupied. Nearby a long incline can be seen stretching to the bottom of the hill. Some quarrying continues, but the empty village shop and the ruined workings further up the hill are a sad reminder of lost prosperity.

In the locality: Titterstone Clee Hill, pages 49 and 88.

Diddlebury

Church of St Peter, page 61.

Eaton-under-Heywood

Church of St Edith, page 61.

Edgmond

Church of St Peter, page 61.

Edstaston

Church of St Mary the Virgin, page 61.

Ellesmere

This small town about 10 miles (16 km) to the east of Oswestry is the unofficial capital of the Shropshire meres, and its main attraction is the largest of these lakes.

The town centre is nondescript but there are some fine timber-framed and Georgian houses on the north side and in Church Street, which leads to the Mere. The church is set impressively on a hill and contains a magnificent south chapel roof and the tomb of Sir Francis Kynaston, Cupbearer to Elizabeth I. Ellesmere was the headquarters of the Ellesmere Canal Company, which promoted an ambitious scheme to link the Severn and the Mersey. The canal wharf and depot are well worth visiting, even if there are few signs of the former pre-eminence of the town, which gave its name to Ellesmere Port (in Cheshire).

The Mere, page 39.

In the locality: Colemere, page 39.

The world's first iron bridge, the centrepiece of the Ironbridge Gorge Museum complex.

Gobowen

See under Oswestry, page 87.

Grinshill

Grinshill is 9 miles (14.5 km) north of Shrews-bury off the A49. The fine pale stone from Grinshill quarries has been known since Roman times and has been used for presti-gious buildings well beyond Shropshire. It is still produced in limited quantities. There are three villages around the hills here. Grinshill itself has an unusual Victorian church in neo-Norman style. The adjacent Higher House and the Elephant and Castle are substantial Georgian houses, but the most interesting building is the Manor, a twin-gabled seven-teenth-century house. Beside the road just outside the village to the east is Stone Grange, acquired in 1617 by Shrewsbury School as a refuge in time of plague. At neighbouring **Clive** the church is unusual for Shropshire in having a spire; it is a Victorian creation, but two Norman doors survive. To the north-east, **Preston Brockhurst** has a notable late Stuart manor house.

In the locality: Corbet Wood, page 39; Moreton Corbet Castle, page 52.

Habberley

See under Pontesbury, page 26.

Hodnet

The church and Hodnet Hall Gardens are the main features of interest, but the visitor should not neglect the village itself, which is unusu-ally large and prosperous-looking. While there are no outstanding buildings, it would be hard to find a Shropshire village with a more rewarding blend of architectural styles.
Church of St Luke, page 61; **Hodnet Hall Gardens**, page 74.

Holdgate

Church of the Holy Trinity, page 62.

Horsehay

Telford Steam Railway, page 88.

Hughley

Church of St John the Baptist, page 62.

Ironbridge

Industrial development in the Severn Gorge during the eighteenth century relied heavily on the river as the principal means of bulk transport in and out of the area, and the gorge was lined with wharves and ferry points. There was also a scattering of labourers' cot-tages, offices and warehouses, but it was not until the construction in 1779 of the world's first iron bridge across the river that a planned settlement grew up on the northern bank, taking its name from the bridge. The layout of the town was governed largely by the difficulty of building on the side of the steep gorge.

Ironbridge now has four distinct areas, reflecting its social and commercial development. The old waterfront extends from the Severn Warehouse (now the Museum of the River) to the bridge, incorporating pubs, former warehouses, shops and small cottages on various levels. At the bridge itself is the planned heart of the town — a little square with pretensions to formality and containing the Tontine Hotel and the big market building, now converted to shops. Bordering the steep Madeley Road at the eastern end of the town is a mainly Victorian area of mixed housing, schools and chapels. Finally, perched above the square, and reached by a steep flight of steps, is St Luke's church, built in the 1830s and the starting point of a nineteenth-century development of gentry houses built on rising levels well above the town. It is a fascinating place, and visitors who baulk at the climbs and confine themselves to the flat riverside area miss a great deal.

On the other side of the bridge an old railway track has been turned into a walk leading to the riverside settlements of Jackfield and Coalport, both of which have museums (page 82).

Ironbridge Gorge Museum (Blists Hill Open Air Museum and **Museum of the River)**, pages 81-2; **Underwater World**, page 84; industrial history, page 85; **Coalbrookdale**, page 16.

In the locality: Buildwas Abbey, page 56; Benthall church and Benthall Hall, pages 59 and 67.

Jackfield
Tile Museum, page 82.

Knockin
See under West Felton, page 34.

Lilleshall
Lilleshall is 3 miles (5 km) south-west of Newport off the A518. In addition to the Abbey, the village is noted for Lilleshall Hall, now the National Sports Centre. Earl Gower, a pioneer industrialist, was responsible for

several early canal works in this area, and enthusiasts can still trace them with the help of specialist publications.

Lilleshall Abbey, page 56.

Little Ness
Adcote house, page 67.

Little Stretton
Church of All Saints, page 63.

Llanyblodwel
This secluded riverside hamlet lies on the extreme western edge of the county (OS 126: SJ 239229). After a visit to the Reverend John Parker's extraordinary church, it is worth strolling down to the river. On the way a bridge with a quaint cautionary warning sign provides a view of Parker's other contributions — the vicarage and school in his own brand of Gothic. Idyllically situated beside the river is a cluster of houses, some timber-framed, with the sixteenth-century Horseshoe Inn at their centre, a charming place for a drink on a summer evening.

Church of St Michael, page 63.

Llanymynech
The industrial history of Llanymynech, 7 miles (11 km) south of Oswestry on the A483, is described on page 85. Together with its neighbour Pant (now largely a dormitory village), it was an important canal and limestone processing centre, and the prosperity of the nineteenth-century years is reflected in some substantial inns and houses in its wide main street, which marks the Welsh border at this point. St Agatha's church of 1845 is a striking experiment in a Norman revival style that failed to become nationally popular. In the heyday of Victorian railways the village was an important junction, and a network of old trackbeds can be traced in the area.

Montgomeryshire Canal, pages 38 and 86; **Llanymynech Hills**, page 42.

In the locality: Offa's Dyke, pages 38 and 49.

Longdon-on-Tern
Aqueduct, page 86.

The Feathers Inn, Ludlow.

Ludlow

Early closing, Thursday; market days,
Monday, Friday and Saturday.

Ludlow is a showpiece among Shropshire towns and several guidebooks with descriptions more detailed than this are available locally. It stands in a strong defensive position, bounded to the south and west by the Teme and to the north by its tributary the Corve, and the castle was always of pre-eminent importance. Its status, and the security it afforded, has conferred prosperity on Ludlow throughout its history.

It achieved early importance as a centre of the wool trade, and in the later middle ages royal connections through the Mortimer family gave it reflected glory. From 1475 it was the seat of the Council of the Marches, the governing body for Wales and the Marches. During the seventeenth and eighteenth centuries it developed steadily as a centre of fashionable life, and much of its later architecture

reflects this period of expansion.

The nucleus of the old town lies at the castle gate. In the twelfth century a broad street ran from here to the Bull Ring, but this space later became occupied by houses, and today the area is a picturesque huddle of buildings and narrow lanes. A walk along this old street is claustrophobic but interesting, with a wide variety of architecture on view. There are no museum pieces here; all the buildings earn their keep, mainly as business premises.

In these narrow thoroughfares it is easy to miss the entrance to the parish church of St Laurence, one of Britain's outstanding churches. Its size, its ambitious architecture and the height of its tower mark it out as a 'wool' church, built on the prosperity derived from the wool trade of the fourteenth and fifteenth centuries. After you have passed through the unusual hexagonal porch, the first impression is of cathedral-like dimensions and soaring height induced by the Perpendicular style, although the spaciousness is a modern phenomenon: originally the vista to the high altar would have been blocked by a more impenetrable screen and the nave would have been cluttered with small chantries.

The church is noted for its stained glass and for the elaborate set of misericords in the chancel stalls. These are a mixture of heraldic symbols, vignettes of medieval life and pure fantasy, and they include a mermaid, a bat with a woman's head-dress, a drinking party and a highway robbery. The great east window is of restored fifteenth-century glass commemorating St Laurence, while the south sanctuary window is unique in portraying six of the Commandments. The reredos under an intricately carved canopy is nineteenth-century work on a grand scale. The Chapel of St John, to the north of the chancel, was the preserve of the Palmers' Guild, a religious body of Ludlow citizens founded in 1250 and later achieving very powerful status. It has some of the best medieval glass, including St Catherine's window to the north and the east window, which portrays a famous legend about Edward the Confessor, adapted here to give it local significance. To the south of the chancel is the Lady Chapel with its own fourteenth-century window.

Two features outside the church should

not be missed. On the north wall is a memorial tablet marking the burial place of the ashes of A. E. Housman, the poet, who though born in Worcestershire did more than anyone else to draw public attention to Shropshire with his collection of poems called *A Shropshire Lad*. The fine thirteenth-century house in the north-east corner of the churchyard was originally erected for the Reader, an assistant to the Rector.

Continuing east from the church entrance, you pass the Buttercross Museum and a splendid group of heavily leaning fifteenth-century buildings at the junction with Broad Street. King Street then runs through to the Bull Ring, which marks the end of the medieval heart of Ludlow. On an island site here is the restored Tolsey, an ancient courthouse. By turning left down Corve Street you reach the celebrated Feathers inn; with its profusion of carved decoration it is much photographed, but its impact is still stunning. The Bull, opposite, is even older though less showy.

The right turn at the Bull Ring is Old Street and not many visitors find their way here. It is a pleasant open thoroughfare notable for a modern development of terraced houses that are a model of sympathetic design. The banks of the Teme at the bottom of the hill are unspoiled, so the crude strength of the fifteenth-century Ludford Bridge shows to fine effect. It is worth making a diversion across the bridge to look at the suburb of Ludford, but the main attraction is the street leading back to the town centre. Lower Broad Street has a pleasing array of small houses, but Broad Street itself, on the other side of the gate, is superb apart from the parked cars. Among a variety of façades, medieval, Georgian and Victorian, the Angel Hotel stands out as an example of an elegant coaching inn. Broad Street was the fashionable centre in the eighteenth century, when every building seems to have been graceful.

Broad Street is almost rivalled by the parallel Mill Street, reached by walking through Bell Lane. By going down to the old Grammar School and along Camp Lane you can reach Dinham, a road which has its own attractive buildings and is a route back to the town centre round the boundary of the old settlement.

Ludlow is a commercial centre, and although the traffic has now been eased by a bypass there still seem to be cars everywhere. So the visitor who wants to see the town at its best is advised to avoid shopping hours. On the other hand the bustling vitality is an indication that Ludlow, like Shrewsbury, wears its antiquity lightly and remains the useful place it has always been.

Castle, page 52; **Buttercross Museum**, page 82.

In the locality: Whitecliffe, page 43; Bromfield bronze age cemetery, page 46; Caynham Camp, page 47; Titterstone Clee Hill, pages 49 and 88; Stokesay Castle, page 53; churches at Richards Castle, page 64, Stanton Lacy, page 64, and Stokesay, page 64; Burford House Gardens, page 71; the Wernlas Collection, Onibury, page 83.

Madeley
Blists Hill Open Air Museum, page 81; see also under Telford and Ironbridge, pages 31 and 18.

Maesbury Marsh
Lying 4 miles (6 km) south-east of Oswestry at OS 126: SJ 314250, the village is the best surviving example in the county of a canal settlement of the early nineteenth century. The little church and chapel, together with several boatmen's cottages (most of them 'improved'), still remain, but the main features of interest are close to the canal bridge and include the Navigation Inn with stabling at the back, a warehouse and a restored wharf with crane.

Montgomeryshire Canal, pages 38 and 87.

Market Drayton
Early closing, Thursday; market day, Wednesday.

In spite of a modern complex in the centre, Market Drayton retains the air of an intimate country town, with random streets full of variegated small-scale architecture. It was a Saxon settlement and gained its market charter as early as 1245, but there is nothing old-world about it. As in other small Shropshire towns, a good many timber-framed structures are concealed by later brick and stucco.

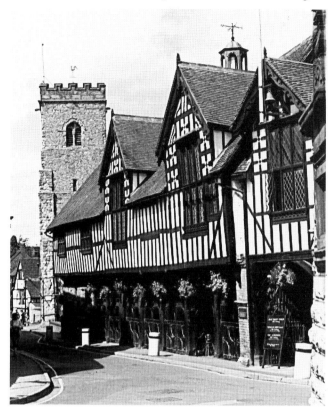

*The Guildhall,
Much Wenlock.*

The Buttercross, an open market hall in Cheshire Street, looks old but dates only from 1824. A turret above it holds the old fire bells. In the streets radiating from here there are several interesting buildings of genuine antiquity. Shropshire Street has the attractive Sandbrook Vaults dating from the mid seventeenth century and the earlier Abbot's House (a very distinctive black and white dwelling, now housing a Chinese restaurant), as well as some of the most impressive Georgian and Victorian architecture. The café and pub at the top of Stafford Street are further good examples of timber framing, while the High Street (more of a small square than a major road) contains the handsome Corbet Arms, a modest coaching inn.

The parish church of St Mary is finely situated on a bank with a steep drop to the south, and its churchyard is a pleasant oasis. There is a good Norman west door, but the interior is solidly Victorian with only occasional older survivals. The tower was the scene of a famous incident in the life of the young Robert Clive, who was educated in the town and caused a stir by climbing out on to one of the gargoyles. His school, rebuilt in 1719, is close to the church on the east side. Great Hales Street, a continuation of the High Street just opposite the school, was once the cattle market and contains some interesting houses, including Townsend House, where the red brick conceals a building dating from about 1500, possibly the oldest in the town.

In the summer there is usually plenty of activity at the canal wharf (page 86), which is about a mile out of town on the Newcastle road (branch left just before the canal bridge).

In the locality: Tyrley Field picnic site, page 40; Hodnet church, page 61; the Dorothy Clive Garden, page 74; Hodnet Hall Gardens, page 74.

Melverley
Church of St Peter, page 63.

Minsterley
Church of the Holy Trinity, page 64.

Moreton Corbet
Castle, page 52.

Morville
Morville Hall, page 75.

Much Wenlock

Early closing, Wednesday.
The A458 Shrewsbury-Bridgnorth road cuts through the edge of Much Wenlock, which is good for the tranquillity of the town but leaves many main-road travellers ignorant of what lies out of sight. What they see in passing is the splendid Gaskell Arms and the top of the High Street, which funnels into a very narrow town centre.

Small though it is, Much Wenlock has an important history. The priory gave it early status, and Edward IV granted a borough charter in 1468, giving the town jurisdiction over a wide area: it returned two MPs until 1885. Its decline was due mainly to the development of industry on its north-eastern side at Ironbridge and Broseley, resulting in a new focus of influence.

Despite the presence of the priory, the Normans built a sizable parish church here. It is light and airy, but of limited interest architecturally, having the scraped look of Victorian restoration. The chapel of St Milburga in the south aisle has been strikingly refurbished in contemporary style, and at the west end is a monument to William Penny Brookes, one of the town's most distinguished residents and a pioneer of the modern revival of the Olympic Games. He had founded a local Olympian Society as early as 1850, and it is still a force in Shropshire athletics, holding its own annual games.

The High Street contains much of interest. At its west end Ashfield Hall is an unusual structure with timber framing incorporated into a stone ground floor. A little further towards the town centre Barclays Bank occupies a black and white house of impressive size, although the most attractive house of this kind is Raynald's Mansion almost opposite, with a finely decorated façade that includes three gables with balconies between. More ambitious is the mid-Victorian Corn Market, which has cavernous archways totally out of scale with the narrow street.

The pride of Much Wenlock is at the centre of the town. The Guildhall is a gem of a building, dating from 1577 and graced with an ornate façade. The ground floor was originally open to accommodate a market place and is now used to house larger museum items. The first-floor chamber is normally open to the public, and the carving is of particular interest. On the opposite street corner the town museum occupies a nineteenth-century memorial hall.

Shineton Street (thus spelt, although the village it refers to is Sheinton) does not seem to attract many visitors. It leads away from the top of the lane to the priory and is the town's most attractive thoroughfare, lined with harmonious houses and cottages in the local stone. It typifies the unassuming archi-

Kynaston's Cave at Nesscliffe.

tecture that makes Much Wenlock such a pleasant place for a relaxed stroll. **Wenlock Priory**, page 57; **Museum**, page 83.

In the locality: Wenlock Edge, page 43; Buildwas Abbey, page 56; churches at Barrow, page 58, Benthall, page 59, Holdgate, page 62, and Hughley, page 62; Benthall Hall, page 67; Shipton Hall, page 75; Wilderhope Manor, page 75; Ironbridge Gorge Museum, page 81.

Nesscliffe

This straggling village on the A5 halfway between Oswestry and Shrewsbury is overshadowed by dramatic red sandstone cliffs containing a cave reputed to be the former lair of Humphrey Kynaston, a sixteenth-century member of a prominent local family who acquired a Robin Hood reputation as a bandit. The fact that his initials are carved into one wall seems a little too good to be true, but it is a pleasant short walk to the cave, starting at a path opposite the Old Three Pigeons. **Nesscliffe Hill Country Park**, page 40. *In the locality: Melverley church, page 63; Adcote house, page 67.*

Newport

Early closing, Thursday; market days, Friday and Saturday.
This is one of Shropshire's most handsome towns, and it makes an instant appeal since most of its outstanding features are displayed in a single sweep of wide main street. It seems to have been a planned Norman town set up as a centre for fishing in the local meres, and it received its borough charter early in the twelfth century. It does not show its age today; there was a great fire in 1665 and comparatively few early buildings have survived. The High Street has a most appealing mixture of Georgian and early Victorian architecture, with some modern replacements successfully designed to blend with their neighbours. The only blot is a brick and glass building on a prominent island site, which partially masks the view of the church behind it.

A convenient starting point for a walk is

the old canal at the north end of the town, where the main road is carried over on a sandstone 'roving bridge', designed to allow horses to cross to a towpath on the opposite side without the need to disconnect the towrope. As you walk back towards the town centre you pass a pleasant terrace of large houses on the right, and the twin almshouses flanking the entrance to the Adams Grammar School of 1656. Here the street divides around St Nicholas's church. Keeping to the left, you pass the Royal Victoria Hotel (unmistakably of the 1830s) and enter St Mary's Street, with its dark granite setts, small shops and the greenery of the churchyard on the other side. It is an attractive thoroughfare, and the vast old Town Hall at its far end comes as something of a surprise. Like many Victorian public buildings, it was designed without regard to the scale of the street, but it looks splendid in Wedgwood blue and white.

St Nicholas's church has the same history as most other urban churches; from modest beginnings it has been altered and enlarged through the centuries and received a comprehensive restoration in the late nineteenth century. The interior is impressive in scale but contains few features of outstanding interest, apart from some pre-Raphaelite glass and a highly ornate reredos.

The harmonious architecture continues on both sides of the High Street, and interesting alleyways lead off from the pavements — a reminder of Newport's medieval origins. There are three striking buildings at the south end of the street. Adams House is classic Georgian in the best style, the old Guildhall is early seventeenth-century (and more attractive for being slightly neglected), while Smallwood Lodge is an oddly rural-looking timber-framed cottage.

Newport needs to be enjoyed slowly and on foot. Much of the architectural appeal is at first-floor level, and it is a town more interesting for its nooks and crannies and odd details than for outstanding buildings.
In the locality: Lilleshall Abbey, page 56; Edgmond church, page 61.

Onibury

The Wernlas Collection, page 83.

Smallwood Lodge Bookshop, Newport.

Oswestry

Early closing, Thursday; market day,
Wednesday (and Saturday in summer).
Tucked away in the north-west of the county
near the Welsh border, Oswestry has suffered
from the warfare of the past. This, together
with one or two disastrous fires, has destroyed
most of the town's early buildings, and its
general character today is Georgian and Victorian. However, in common with other
Shropshire towns, Oswestry has several structures of the sixteenth and seventeenth centuries concealed behind brick or stucco façades.

The parish church of St Oswald is imposing but undistinguished architecturally,
having been substantially rebuilt in the seventeenth and nineteenth centuries. Within the
churchyard boundary is Holbache House, the
former town grammar school, dating originally from 1407 but altered from Tudor times,
while at the adjacent crossroads the building
which includes the Coach and Dogs restaurant is of the mid seventeenth century. This
end of Church Street is dominated by the
handsome late Georgian frontage of the
Wynnstay Arms and the fine town mansion

called Bellan House; these large buildings,
together with the wide main street and the
nearby Cae Glas park, contribute to an air of
spaciousness, which quickly disappears as the
street funnels into the town centre at the Cross.
Here the close huddle of shops and offices is
predominantly Victorian, and the well preserved Llwyd Mansion of 1604 stands out
rather incongruously among its neighbours.

The Mansion stands at the narrow entrance
to Bailey Street, which contains an interesting variety of small-scale architecture of many
dates. It leads to the Bailey Head, a square
given over on Wednesdays to a large street
market that has the merit of distracting attention from the unfortunate 'new' market hall,
squatting uneasily next to a fine Victorian
Guildhall. As the name implies, this area
once lay within the boundary of the castle,
and the motte behind the Guildhall can still be
climbed although only fragments of the
masonry remain.

From here a walk down the narrow Arthur
Street brings you into Willow Street. It looks
undistinguished at first glance but is lined
by some good examples of substantial

nineteenth-century town houses converted to other uses. The crossroads halfway up is the site of one of the town gates, and it is worth turning left into Welsh Walls and following the road round past the park and the church into Upper Brook Street. This road and its continuation below the traffic lights contain a pleasing blend of buildings spanning at least three centuries.

On the other side of the town, Beatrice Street should not be missed. It is reached from the Bailey Head via Albion Hill. The true age of many of the buildings here is hidden by brick frontages, but the timber-framed shop on the left was once the Fighting Cocks Inn and still retains its original appearance.

Oswestry has always flourished as a market town, and some of its distinctive atmosphere disappeared when the cattle market was removed to a modern site on the south-east outskirts. The bleak central car park now occupies the old site, but although the cattle are out of sight Wednesdays are still marked by a bustle and conviviality.

Old Oswestry iron age settlement, page 49; **Heritage and Exhibition Centre**, page 83; **Transport Museum**, page 83; **Park Hall Working Farm Museum**, page 83; industrial history, page 87.

In the locality: Montgomeryshire Canal, pages 38 and 86; Offa's Dyke, pages 38 and 49; Cefn Coch picnic site, page 40; Llanymynech Hills, page 42; Oswestry Old Racecourse, page 42; Wat's Dyke, page 50; Whittington Castle, page 54; Selattyn church, page 64.

Pant

Montgomeryshire Canal, page 87.

Pontesbury

Once a small village of ancient origin, 7 miles (11 km) south-west of Shrewsbury on the A488, Pontesbury has in recent years been scheduled as a centre of development, and the novelist Mary Webb, who lived here for a short time, would have difficulty in recognising it now. The large church stands at the highest point of the village and is of limited architectural interest, with a nave and tower of 1829 added to the thirteenth-century chan-

cel after a collapse in 1825. There is now little sign of the small-scale industrial activity — mainly coal mining and lead processing — that once took place on the eastern outskirts of Pontesbury, which was also a railhead for the Snailbeach lead mines. The short drive south to **Habberley**, a hamlet with a small church and timber-framed hall, is well worth while.

In the locality: Earl's Hill, page 39; Poles Coppice, page 40; Minsterley church, page 64; Snailbeach, page 88.

Preston Brockhurst

See under Grinshill, page 18.

Preston upon the Weald Moors

Hoo Farm Country Park, page 84.

Quatford

This small settlement, just off the A442 2 miles (3 km) from Bridgnorth, is of interest because Domesday Book showed it as the only Shropshire borough apart from Shrewsbury. Its importance was due to its bridge across the Severn, but this advantage was lost when a new bridge was constructed at Bridgnorth in about 1100. It is worth visiting the church on its prominent rock to see the early Norman chancel. At **Quatt**, 3 miles (5 km) further down the road, the church is of architectural interest and has some good monuments. Opposite is the Dower House, of the early eighteenth century.

In the locality: Dudmaston Hall, page 74.

Quatt

See under Quatford, above; Dudmaston Hall, page 74.

Richards Castle

Church of All Saints, page 64.

Rushbury

Rushbury (OS 138: SO 514919) is one of the larger hamlets that lie under the western slopes of Wenlock Edge. Its centre is a very pleasant group comprising the church, the school and the former vicarage. St Peter's church is of interest, with a late Norman chancel, herringbone masonry in the nave and fine roof timbers. The adjacent school dates from 1821 and has the pleasing style of that time. A short distance down the lane is the Manor, a splendid timber-framed house with three symmetrical gables and a substantial stone chimney.

In the locality: Wenlock Edge, page 43; churches at Eaton-under-Heywood, page 61, and Holdgate, page 62; Wilderhope Manor, page 75.

Ruyton-Eleven-Towns

Situated between Oswestry and Baschurch, Ruyton is a long, rambling village built along two streets at right angles to each other on a hill. It is a good example of an unprettified village with many buildings constructed of the local sandstone and showing a wide variety of vernacular styles. The characteristic feature is the use of very large blocks with some timber framing behind the solid façades. The village got its unusual name when eleven townships were united in the manor of Ruyton, which became a borough in 1301 and survived as such until 1883. Very little remains of the castle but the twelfth-century church retains some of its original work.

Selattyn

Church of St Mary, page 64.

Shifnal

Early closing, Thursday.

Shifnal was once an important staging post on the Holyhead Road. Its centre consists of a main street lined with shops and heavily overhung by an inelegant railway bridge. There is one outstanding building in the commercial area — the Nell Gwyn, a large timber-framed public house, standing to the east of the bridge and beautifully restored in the modern fashion without black gloss paint. Old Idsall House, a building smaller but of similar character, has survived at the church gate in a more or less unrestored condition.

Although Shifnal has never been much more than an expanded village it has a church of cathedral-like proportions, with a lofty and handsome hammerbeam roof. An unusual feature is the parvise or small room over the entrance, probably used as a schoolroom. A lack of clear glass makes the nave dark, but the gloom serves to show off a series of windows in the north wall, installed as a First World War memorial and depicting the various stages of a knight's service. A rare architectural feature is the survival of the Norman chancel arch next to the later fourteenth-century arch, and even more unusual is the fact that the Norman arch has at its head a pagan 'green man' carving. Other outstanding features are a carved Italian pulpit of the seventeenth century, an exotic Victorian reredos (also from Italy) and a set of panels behind the organ recording various feats of bellringing.

In the locality: Nedge Hill picnic site, page 40; Lilleshall Abbey, page 56; White Ladies Priory, page 57; Tong church, page 66; Boscobel House, page 70; Weston Park, page 75; Aerospace Museum, page 79.

Shipton

Shipton Hall, page 75.

Shrewsbury

Market days, Tuesday and Friday.

For most visitors to Shrewsbury the first question will be where to park. The old town centre is intricate and constricted, and it is advisable to cross the Welsh Bridge and turn right into the big Frankwell car park. From here a pedestrian footbridge crosses the river to the main shopping centre, but a walk back to the Welsh Bridge makes a good start to a tour of the town.

The river Severn has always been important to Shrewsbury. It makes a dramatic meander here and forms a wide loop that fails by only a few hundred yards to become a complete circle; within this natural moat the old town was built. In later years the river was an important means of transport; today its banks provide the town's major recreational area.

Before crossing the bridge, look at the buildings on the Frankwell side. Frankwell developed very early as a busy suburb outside the town walls and it has its own distinct history and personality. It is possible to see here one of the most attractive aspects of Shrewsbury — the way in which old buildings have been adapted for modern commercial use in unselfconscious ways.

On the other side of the bridge the prospect

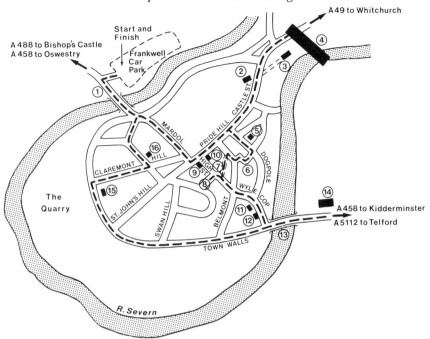

A49 to Whitchurch

Start and Finish

A 488 to Bishop's Castle
A 458 to Oswestry

Frankwell Car Park

MARDOL

PRIDE HILL

CASTLE ST

DOGPOLE

CLAREMONT

HILL

HIGH ST

WYLE COP

The Quarry

ST JOHN'S HILL

SWAN HILL

BELMONT

TOWN WALLS

R. Severn

A458 to Kidderminster
A5112 to Telford

Shrewsbury; 1 Welsh Bridge; 2 Public Library (formerly Shrewsbury School); 3 Castle; 4 Station; 5 St Mary's church; 6 Bear Steps, St Alkmund's, St Julian's, Abbots House; 7 Grope Lane; 8 The Square; 9 Ireland's Mansion; 10 Owen's Mansion; 11 Lion Hotel; 12 Mytton's Mansion; 13 English Bridge; 14 Abbey Church; 15 St Chad's church; 16 Rowley's House.

at first seems unpromising as you confront a jumble of undistinguished architecture, but by turning left, crossing the road and walking up Mardol you experience for the first time the narrow, lively streets and huddled buildings that have defied the planners over the years. The dramatically leaning King's Head is the most eye-catching of a whole range of façades that keep the eye firmly at first-floor level. At the top of Mardol cross the little pedestrian area and turn left into Pride Hill. This is the bottom of the main shopping street and again an extraordinary variety of buildings has been pressed into service as modern shops.

Pride Hill levels off to become Castle Street, where the big chain stores on the left are the only evidence of the twentieth century establishing a brief dominance. Even so, on the other side of the road there is another fascinating jumble of frontages. The Jacobean timber framing of one shop compares

oddly with the Victorian imitation that houses its near neighbour. Some of the fakery is impressive: note the early twentieth-century Co-operative store and the large Presbyterian church in neo-Norman style just beyond. Tucked away between these two buildings is a Jacobean gateway with elaborate carved woodwork. It leads to a tranquil courtyard and the old Council House, once the meeting place of the Council of the Welsh Marches.

Castle Street drops sharply at this point, but a path on the right carries straight on past Castle Gates House (seventeenth-century, but moved here from Dogpole in 1702) to the castle entrance. The castle houses the Shropshire Regimental Museum. To the left is the public library of Grinshill stone. It formed the premises of Shrewsbury School before the school moved out to Kingsland in 1882, and it is fronted by a dignified statue of Charles Darwin, one of the most distinguished former pupils.

Continue down the hill and turn right up some steps into a passageway called The Dana, which leads across the railway lines and brings you out opposite the prison. This features darkly in several of A. E. Housman's poems but is an attractive building designed with typical elegance by Thomas Telford. Almost next to it down the hill is a magnificent warehouse marking the old canal terminal. Back in Castle Gates it is only a few yards to one of Britain's finest provincial railway stations, built in Tudor style.

Walk back up Castle Street on the other side of the road past the public library and take the right turn beside Halford's shop. It leads to School Gardens and a very interesting group of seventeenth-century and Georgian houses. At the top of Pride Hill turn left into St Mary's Street. The church on the left is the oldest in the town centre, and apart from its architectural interest is notable for the finest assemblage of stained glass in the county — gathered mainly from European sources by a nineteenth-century incumbent. The great east window of about 1350 was moved here when the old church of St Chad collapsed in 1788. A walk round the church 'close' reveals some fine timber-framed buildings, including the Drapers' Hall, St Mary's Cottages and the Olde Yorkshire House (now brick-faced).

A few yards further along St Mary's Street a right turn into Church Street brings you to the oasis of St Alkmund's Place. Two churches with spires stand almost side by side here. St Alkmund's itself was largely rebuilt in the late eighteenth century and incorporates some cast-iron work, while St Julian's has now been converted into a crafts centre. The restored group of medieval buildings in the middle of St Alkmund's Place is the Bear Steps Hall, the oldest part of which dates from the fourteenth century. Butcher Row, leading from here to Pride Hill, contains the superb fifteenth-century Abbot's House.

On the lower side of Bear Steps, Grope Lane, one of Shrewsbury's characteristic alleyways (or 'shuts') descends to the High Street. You emerge opposite the Square, a pleasant pedestrian area dominated by the Market Hall of 1595. To your right, at the junction of High Street and Pride Hill, two of the town's best timber-framed buildings face

each other. They are both of the late sixteenth century. Owen's Mansion is occupied by Owen Owen's store, while opposite is Ireland's Mansion, probably the most spectacular urban black and white house in the county. Both were built by rich wool merchants.

Now walk away from the Square along the High Street to the point where it descends steeply into Wyle Cop. The fine coaching inn on the right is the Lion Hotel and just beyond it is the remarkable first-floor façade of Mytton's Mansion, notable for the variety of its windows, including one with intricate tracery. The road now leads to the English Bridge, with the Abbey Church prominent on the other side. Virtually nothing remains of the other abbey buildings, although a refectory pulpit stands isolated opposite the church on the other side of the road. The abbey was founded by Roger de Montgomery in 1083 for the Benedictines, but the present church is a mixture of styles. The most prominent feature, the west tower, is of the fourteenth century and so is its splendid window, which was added later. The nave contains the oldest

Bear Steps, Shrewsbury.

St Chad's church, Shrewsbury.

portions of the church, the massive pillars and arcade, which belonged to the original structure. The chancel is almost entirely the result of restoration in 1886 by John Pearson, who also designed the east window and elaborate reredos.

The final stage of the walk is along the town walls, reached by returning over the bridge and taking the left turn at the bottom of Wyle Cop. This road runs high above the river, with views across playing fields and the park known as the Quarry to Shrewsbury School on the opposite bank. There is now an abrupt change to Georgian and Victorian architecture, because this area was favoured by wealthy residents of the eighteenth and early nineteenth centuries. The first notable building is the small mid-Victorian Roman Catholic cathedral, and just beyond it to the right Belmont contains examples of the best Georgian building styles. Further along, the Ear, Nose and Throat Hospital provides a rare instance in Shrewsbury of a major nineteenth-century structure, but the gem of the town walls area is the 'new' St Chad's church, a view of which appears as the road widens.

When the original St Chad's collapsed in 1788 (the ruins can be seen in Princess Street) George Steuart, the architect of Attingham Hall, was commissioned to build a new church on this commanding site. He produced a most unusual design consisting of a west tower of classical inspiration and an ante-chamber leading into a large circular nave. The west façade has an elegant portico. As in most churches of this date, the chancel and nave are integrated, though the sanctuary is marked out by heavy columns. Everything else is light and airy, an effect made possible by restrained ornamentation and the use of cast iron for the slendar pillars of the gallery. Unfortunately the interior was not improved by the addition of Victorian stained glass.

Just beyond the church Claremont Hill leads down into Barker Street and from there it is a short distance back to the Welsh Bridge.

Castle, page 53; **Battlefield church**, page 59; **Clive House Museum**, page 83; **Coleham Pumping Station**, page 85; **Rowley's House Museum**, page 83; **Shropshire Regimental Museum**, page 84; industrial history, page 88.

In the locality: Earl's Hill, page 39; Lyth Hill, page 40; Nesscliffe Hill Country Park, page 40; Viroconium Roman City and Museum, page 49; Acton Burnell Castle, page 51; Moreton Corbet Castle, page 52; Haughmond Abbey, page 56; churches at Acton Burnell, page 58, Atcham, page 58, Condover, page 60, Melverley, page 63, and Minsterley, page 64; Langley Chapel, page 63; Adcote house, page 67; Attingham Park, page 67; Condover Hall, page 71.

Snailbeach

Industrial history, page 88.

Stanton Lacy

Church of St Peter, page 64.

Stokesay

Castle, page 53; church of St John the Baptist, page 64.

Stottesdon

Church of St Mary, page 66.

Telford

In order to understand Telford New Town it is necessary to look at its history. It originated as an imaginative idea in the 1960s that the worked-out Shropshire coalfield, which had left a desolate wasteland that was useless for agriculture, would be a very suitable site for a new town, perhaps even a city. The additional population was to come from the West Midlands conurbation, at that time the most prosperous industrial region in Britain, and industry to employ the migrants was to be attracted from the same area.

Originally the town was to be named after Dawley, which was to be incorporated into the new creation along with other established settlements like Wellington, Hadley, Oakengates and Madeley. However, it was felt that a neutral name would be more appropriate, and the decision was made to commemorate Thomas Telford, who had left his mark throughout Shropshire.

Because of successive phases of economic recession Telford's subsequent history has not gone entirely to plan. Sophisticated modern industries have been attracted here, but not in sufficient number or variety to prevent unemployment. As with other new towns, there are complaints that the environment is not 'people-friendly'.

On the other hand there have been significant achievements. A great many people are living in pleasanter surroundings than they knew before. An ugly landscape has been transformed, and large areas of wasteland are now put to beneficial use for recreational purposes. The huge Town Park, part urban, part rural, is an imaginative project. Old residential areas suffering from post-industrial decay have been revitalised — notably in the Ironbridge area described on pages 18 and 85.

For the visitor interested in sociology there is much of interest here, but visual pleasures are rare. At the northern end the old centre of Wellington is still worth looking at for its huddled shopping streets (see separate entry, page 32).

To the south, the area around **Madeley** church has been preserved, and the old vicarage here is perhaps the most interesting building in Telford; dating from 1700, it has most of its front windows bricked up but remains supremely elegant. The church itself is in the characteristic style of Thomas Telford. The nearby Old Hall Barn is a fine structure mer-

The old vicarage, Madeley.

cifully left alone, but Madeley Hall, at the top of Church Street, a Queen Anne house with a complex of outbuildings, has been so ruthlessly renovated that its character has virtually disappeared. It should not be confused with Madeley Court, an isolated mansion about half a mile (800 metres) to the north of Madeley centre. Basically medieval with many later accretions, it can be visited by the general public.

A network of footpaths runs through Telford and maps are available locally.

Hoo Farm Country Park, page 84; **Telford Steam Railway**, page 88; **Ironbridge Gorge Museum**, page 81; industrial history, page 88.

In the locality: Granville Country Park, page 40; Nedge Hill picnic site, page 40; The Wrekin, pages 43 and 50; Buildwas Abbey, page 56; Lilleshall Abbey, page 56; Benthall church, page 59; Benthall Hall, page 67; Underwater World, page 84.

Tong

Church of St Mary the Virgin with St Bartholomew, page 66; White Ladies Priory, page 57; Boscobel House, page 70; Weston Park, page 75.

Upton Cressett

Upton Cressett Hall, page 75.

Wellington

Now part of the new town of Telford, Wellington still retains the air of a Victorian market town, with its narrow pedestrianised streets and harmonious buildings. All Saints, on an elevated site, is one of the few classical churches in Shropshire. It was designed by George Steuart, whose more famous creation was St Chad's in Shrewsbury. The exterior is eighteenth-century and the interior sumptuously Victorian, with marble columns supporting its galleries, an imposing organ and brilliant colour in the east window.

In the locality: The Wrekin, pages 43 and 50; Telford Steam Railway, page 88; Longdon-on-Tern aqueduct, page 86.

Welsh Frankton

Montgomeryshire Canal locks, page 86.

Wem

Market days, Tuesday, Thursday and Saturday.

Wem is another of the small Shropshire towns of no particular style or period. It is a placid rural centre for shopping and useful services. It was created as an adjunct to a castle, but later redevelopment and a disastrous fire in the seventeenth century have left few medieval traces. For a small town it has a surprising number of distinguished associations (see chapter 10). William Hazlitt lived here as a boy (his first published piece was a letter to the *Shrewsbury Chronicle*) and when the notorious Judge Jeffreys was ennobled he took the title Baron Jeffreys of Wem and bought Lowe Hall to the north-west of the town. Another resident was William Betty, famous in theatrical history as a child actor who became a cult figure in late eighteenth-century London.

Hazlitt's house in Noble Street is marked by a plaque, and in the same street stands the celebrated Wem Brewery, occupying a group of old buildings. Further along, the Conservative Club is a fine example of a late Georgian provincial town house. The High Street has little architectural distinction although the Castle Inn stands out pleasantly.

The church is right in the centre of the town — an oddly assorted building with a tower that is basically fourteenth-century, a nave of the early nineteenth century and a Victorian chancel. The mixture is more noticeable inside, where the plain, almost puritanical nave contrasts strangely with the highly ornamented chancel. The latter was refurbished and embellished in 1886 by the rector of the time, and the results include a low marble and wrought iron screen with gates, an elaborate carved reredos and a rare example of a wrought-iron pulpit. The two large brass chandeliers are believed to date from the 1730s.

In the locality: Corbet Wood, page 39;

(Opposite) John Gwynne's bridge at Atcham.

Moreton Corbet Castle, page 52; Edstaston church, page 61.

West Felton

The village, 5 miles (8 km) south-east of Oswestry, is split by the new Oswestry by-pass, and access is by the old A5, which runs parallel. The church has a good Norman nave, and just to the west of it is an over-grown castle motte of the same period. A cluster of harmonious buildings, most of them modernised and converted, makes up the old village centre. Down the lane to the south-west, at **Woolston**, is St Winifred's Well, reputedly the spot where the saint's bones rested on the journey between Holywell, Clwyd, and Shrewsbury. The tiny timber-framed cottage here has been renovated by the Landmark Trust. **Knockin**, to the south of West Felton, is another pleasantly strag-gling village with an interesting church and a motte.

In the locality: Montgomeryshire Canal, pages 38 and 86.

The Talbot Memorial in St Alkmund's church, Whitchurch.

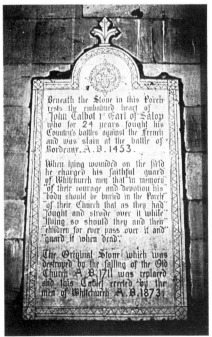

Weston-under-Redcastle (Hawkstone Park)

Weston, 14 miles (22.5 km) north of Shrews-bury off the A49, is an attractive village in itself, but it is better known for its proximity to Hawkstone Park. The impressive Hawkstone Hall was built for Sir Richard Hill in the early eighteenth century. (Now a reli-gious college, it is open to the public on occasional days in the summer.) Later in the century the Hills set out to create what may well have been the first theme park, with a series of 'romantic' attractions, such as Gothic ruins, a hermit's grotto and an 'Awful Preci-pice'. It drew a host of distinguished visitors, and the remains can be seen today, although it is necessary to enter by way of the Hawkstone Park Hotel and Golf Club, which also occu-pies the site. (Avoid trespassing on the golf course.)

In the locality: Moreton Corbet Castle, page 52; Hodnet church, page 61; Hodnet Hall Gardens, page 74.

Whitchurch

Early closing, Wednesday; market day, Friday.

Whitchurch is Shropshire's northern outpost, almost on the county boundary, with Che-shire to the north and an odd pocket of Wales to the west. It is the one town in Shropshire that can claim with certainty to have been built on a Roman site; the town of *Mediolanum* has been identified here, al-though traces of it are negligible. The town has no obvious showpieces apart from the church, but its range of highly individual Georgian and Victorian buildings are a de-light to the connoisseur and impress the casual visitor with their unpretentious charm.

The tall tower of St Alkmund's church dominates the High Street. It has the spaci-ousness and light of the early eighteenth cen-tury, although the Victorian restorers added gloomy stained glass at the east end, out of keeping with the rest of the interior. In the sanctuary is the tomb of John Talbot, Earl of Shrewsbury, who died in France in 1453. Photographs at the tomb illustrate what was found when the bones were disinterred in 1874. On the other side of the church is the effigy of John Talbot, who founded the local grammar school in 1550.

The nineteenth-century mock Elizabethan building that last housed the Grammar School can be seen near the church in Bargates. Next to it is a tiny infants' school of 1708 and the Higginson Almshouses, a most attractive row of Georgian cottages. A walk down the High Street reveals some interesting shop frontages. The black and white Bear Inn at the top is not as old as it looks, and the unassuming garage opposite is believed to be much older. A little way down on the right, the rather shabby Victoria Hotel looks more appealing than many over-restored pubs, while the shop almost next door has superb cast-iron decoration (it used to be the premises of J. B. Joyce, the famous clockmakers). The town's most obviously impressive building, the National Westminster Bank at the bottom of the hill, is a fake, having been built in blatant imitation Tudor in the 1930s.

St Mary's Lane turns off the High Street almost opposite the bank, and a little way along is a pub called the Old Town Hall Vaults, the birthplace of the composer Edward German. The High Street turns sharply right at the bottom and reaches the junction of several roads. From here Watergate Street leads into Dodington, once the exclusive quarter of Whitchurch. Apart from a wealth of handsome houses there is the disused church of St Catherine, a most elegant structure of 1836. The walk back to the church can take in the pleasant Jubilee Park to the south of the town.

In the locality: Brown Moss, page 39.

Whittington

A bypass has brought peace to this large village on the eastern outskirts of Oswestry, and its centre is now a pleasant place in which to park and picnic. The castle is the dominant feature, its moat providing what is virtually a village pond. The nearby church is basically of the later eighteenth century but received much Victorian attention — one result being the remarkable unsupported span of its interior. A notable incumbent here was William Walsham How, later Bishop of Wakefield, who wrote many hymns, including 'For all the Saints' (see chapter 10). Next to the church is a substantial seventeenth-century manor house, and a walk round the village will reveal an interesting mixture of small Georgian and Victorian buildings.

Castle, page 54.

Woolston

See under West Felton, page 34.

Woore

There is always some doubt as to whether Woore, just on the county border 7 miles (11 km) north-east of Market Drayton, is really a Shropshire village — its natural association is with Newcastle-under-Lyme and Stoke-on-Trent. It is a pleasant place, with two good buildings facing each other. One is St Leonard's church, built in 1830 in an elegant classical style and cased in white stucco. The other is the Swan Hotel, probably of Tudor origin but given a new façade in the 1820s as a coaching inn.

In the locality: the Dorothy Clive Garden, page 74.

Worfield

Worfield is the estate village of Davenport House and is situated 4 miles (6.5 km) north-east of Bridgnorth. The large church has a complex building history that has produced a very impressive interior, and from its elevated site there is a view of Lower House, a fine timber-framed structure of two distinct periods. The village itself is a charming blend of unpretentious houses of several periods, well worth a leisurely stroll.

In the locality: Claverley church, page 60.

Wroxeter

Viroconium Roman City and Museum, page 49.

The Navigation Inn at Maesbury Marsh.

(Opposite) A waterfall in Carding Mill Valley.

3
The Shropshire countryside

The modern trend towards 'organised access' to the countryside is becoming evident in Shropshire. Nature reserves and picnic sites have been designated, and an extensive network of footpaths has been signposted and waymarked. Tourist information centres now provide details of guided walks and a generous choice of leaflets for the benefit of walkers, although many people will prefer to find their own way around with the aid of the excellent 1:25,000 Ordnance Survey maps, which show footpaths very clearly. This chapter contains a selection of short outings and longer expeditions on land freely accessible to the public.

Long-distance footpaths

The Montgomeryshire Canal towpath

This is not technically a right of way but can be used on sufferance. The Shropshire stretch is clear and walking is easy. The main canal features to be seen are described on page 86, and there is a good deal of botanical and wildlife interest. Complete restoration of the canal is under discussion and would change its character; at the time of writing it is normally deserted, except perhaps in the Queen's Head area, where a network of subsidiary walks has been waymarked (pamphlet available from Oswestry information centre). The northern starting point is Frankton Junction (OS 126: SJ 371318) and the Welsh border is reached at Llanymynech (OS 126: SJ 266210). Convenient access points are Rednal (OS 126: SJ 352277), Queen's Head (OS 126: SJ 339268) and Maesbury Marsh (OS 126: SJ 314250).

Offa's Dyke Path

This is the second-longest and the most varied of Britain's official long-distance paths, extending from Prestatyn to Chepstow. The Shropshire stretch is rugged enough to be interesting yet feasible for an active family. The most interesting lengths are detailed in the section on the Dyke on page 49. The path is clearly marked on up-to-date Ordnance Survey maps and well defined on the ground, and additional information is contained in pamphlets produced by the Countryside Commission and available from information centres along the route. Anyone contemplating an extended walk will find a wealth of information about the Dyke and the footpath at the Offa's Dyke Centre, The Old School, Knighton, Powys.

The Shropshire Way

This is a circular walk, entirely on public rights of way, devised largely by local members of the Ramblers' Association and taking in some of the remotest and most scenic Shropshire countryside as well as some historic towns. Its maximum length is about 170 miles (275 km). It starts in the north near Whitchurch and passes through Wem, the Wrekin, Much Wenlock, the Clee Hills, Ludlow, Clun, the Long Mynd and Shrewsbury. A comprehensive guide by Robert Kirk is published by the Thornhill Press and can be bought in local bookshops, but the path is not always waymarked and an Ordnance Survey map is essential.

Countryside leisure areas

Bog Mine, Pennerley (OS 137: SO 356979)

This former lead and zinc mine near the Stiperstones is now reclaimed. There are many industrial remains and part of the site is a nature conservation area. It can be reached by heading south from Minsterley on the A488, then turning left on the minor road passing through Snailbeach and Pennerley for about 6 miles (10 km).

Brown Clee (OS 138: SO 607873)

This is an area of moor and woodland near the top of Shropshire's highest hill. There are

A length of the Offa's Dyke long-distance footpath near Selattyn.

footpaths to the summit at over 1700 feet (520 metres). Car access is signposted from Cleobury North on the B4364 Bridgnorth to Ludlow road.

Brown Moss (OS 126: SJ 563393)

This comprises 80 acres (32 hectares) of heath, woodland and marsh of considerable botanical interest. The simplest access is from the A41 2¹/₂ miles (4 km) south of Whitchurch; the turning is at SJ 555385.

Colemere (OS 126: SJ 436329)

Colemere is a lake 3 miles (5 km) south-east of Ellesmere. It is reached by a minor road off the A528; a pleasant alternative is to walk along the canal towpath from the road junction at SJ 414340 (OS 126). The 68 acre (28 hectare) mere is surrounded by extensive woodland, with picnic places and plenty of opportunities for walking.

Corbet Wood (OS 126: SJ 525238)

This area, 3 miles (5 km) south of Wem, is close to the famous Grinshill quarries, and the woodland walks are made more interesting by the overgrown red sandstone outcrops. There are fine views to the south.

Earl's Hill (OS 126: SJ 410049)

This site to the south-west of Shrewsbury provides some strenuous walking and panoramic views of the border country from a height of about 1000 feet (300 metres). There is no close access by car; the nearest parking place is the filling station at Pontesford on the A488 at SJ 408063, where a lane leads off the road to the hill. A detailed guide to wildlife and natural features is published by the Shropshire Conservation Trust; the pamphlet also provides a useful guide to what can be seen from the summit.

Edge Wood (OS 137: SO 478877)

This is a remote spot on Wenlock Edge between Harton and Westhope. It can be reached from the B4368 by a turning 4 miles (6 km) east of Craven Arms or from the B4371 at Hope Bowdler, near Church Stretton. The site lies in the belt of trees that runs the length of Wenlock Edge, but short walks lead to fine views of the countryside to the north and south of the ridge. The Shropshire Conservation Trust publishes a trail.

Ellesmere: The Mere (OS 126: SJ 405347)

This is the largest and most accessible of

the lakes in the area. It lies beside the A528 on the southern edge of the town and is notable for the many kinds of waterfowl to be seen. A visitors' centre provides information about these and other aspects of the district's natural history. It is possible to walk through woodland part of the way round the Mere and boats can be hired in the summer from a landing stage in the neighbouring Cremorne Gardens.

Granville Country Park, Donnington Wood, Telford (OS 127: SJ 712124) (close to junction of B4373 and B5060).

Well-made paths offer a variety of walks through this area of grassland and woodland. Information panels point out wildlife features and also evidence of former industrial activity, including coal mining and canal works. There are no visitor facilities.

Lyth Hill (OS 126: SJ 477072)

The site is an area of grassland, scrub and woodland with outstanding views of neighbouring hills and excellent walking opportunities. It is about 4 miles (6 km) south of Shrewsbury, west of the A49 just beyond Bayston Hill.

Nesscliffe Hill Country Park (OS 126: SJ 385195).

Nesscliffe Hill is a prominent sandstone escarpment accessible off the A5 midway between Oswestry and Shrewsbury. Fine views, old quarries, walks through mixed woodland and a cave reputedly used by the highwayman Humphrey Kynaston are among the attractions.

Poles Coppice, Pontesbury (OS 126: SJ 393048 and SJ 385042)

The site, 1 1/2 miles (2 km) south of Pontesbury, comprises 50 acres (20 hectares) including former quarry workings and very old woodland of great interest to naturalists. There are good short walks.

Rectory Wood (OS 137: SO 446938)

This 16 acre (6.5 hectare) site was established by the county council in the former grounds of the Old Rectory at Church Stretton as a conservation area for traditional wood-

land. It lies on the outskirts of the town just below the Long Mynd and can be reached on foot by walking up Burway Road and taking a path to the left by the cattle grid.

Picnic sites

The following are recommended as brief stops during a car tour or as starting points for short and not too arduous walks.

Cefn Coch (OS 126: SJ 242329)

This Forestry Commission site in a remote and peaceful area to the west of Oswestry and close to the Welsh border is reached by taking the B4580 out of Oswestry, turning right at the Old Racecourse and left after 1 mile (1.6 km) at Carreg-y-Byg, where the route crosses Offa's Dyke.

Colstey Bank (OS 137: SO 305841)

A Forestry Commission site in a deserted area 3 miles (5 km) north of Clun off the A488, this area of woodland contains the Bury Ditches hillfort (see page 46).

Hawkbatch (OS 138: SO 761778)

This Forestry Commission site is on the extreme south-east border of Shropshire in the Wyre Forest. Access is from the B4194 between Bewdley and Bridgnorth. Among the extensive forest walks is one leading to the banks of the river Severn.

Nedge Hill (OS 127: SJ 717073)

This picnic place is 3 miles (5 km) west of Shifnal and is accessible from the A464 or the A4169. It lies in high woodland with good views to the east and west.

Tyrley Field (OS 127: SJ 677337)

Off the A529 1 mile (1.6 km) south of Market Drayton, the site has walks connecting with the towpath of the Shropshire Union Canal, which is always busy in the summer months.

Opportunities for longer walks

Included here are areas which are accessible by car but which provide the chance of longer

The Wrekin.

rambles, mainly in hill country. Ordnance Survey maps (the 1:50,000 series or, better, the 1:25,000 sheets) are necessary. Ramblers should also bear in mind the possibilities offered by the iron age hillforts described in chapter 4.

Carding Mill Valley

The valley is a deep ravine running into the Long Mynd north of Church Stretton. It is National Trust property and accessible by car via a turning off the B4370 at SO 454942 (OS 137). Refreshments and information are available just over half a mile (800 metres) up the lane. It is a pleasant place for picnicking by the stream and can be over-popular on fine summer days, but there is no difficulty in escaping from the crowds by taking one of the many walks up to the Long Mynd (see below).

Hopesay Hill

This is a fine stretch of National Trust property on the eastern fringes of the Clun Forest, and 2 miles (3 km) west of Craven Arms. There are three main points of access where cars may be left: at Aston-on-Clun (OS 137: SO 394820), at Hopesay village (OS 137: SO 391835) or near Wart Hill at the northern end (OS 137: SO 402845). The hill consists of open heathland and sheep pasture at over 1000 feet (300 metres) and there are magnificent views in all directions.

Llanymynech Hills

This range stands beside the A483, 4 miles (6 km) south of Oswestry. Although not high by some standards, the hills rise sharply from low-lying land and provide exceptional views over the Severn valley to the east and into the Tanat valley to the west. They include a section of Offa's Dyke, and walkers can follow the long-distance path on the western side. The Romans had copper mines here, and the limestone has been heavily quarried in more recent years; the disused workings add considerable interest to the hills at the Llanymynech end (see page 85). Access is either from Llynclys at the lane leading from the A495 at SJ 277242 (OS 126) or from Llanymynech, at the lane from the A483 at SJ 266213.

Long Mynd

The Long Mynd (pronounced to rhyme with 'tinned') is an extensive area of high and deserted moorland to the south-west of Shrewsbury. The plateau is broken on the eastern side by a series of 'batches' or 'hollows' — deep ravines running down to the Stretton valley. It is possible to drive on the unfenced roads shown on the Ordnance Survey map and to stop at many points for short walks. A recommended drive starts at Leebotwood (OS 137: SO 476987) along the minor road through Woolstaston and Ratlinghope and then back across the top to Church Stretton. There are dozens of longer walks, many of them passing up the various hollows to the Port Way, an ancient track running the length of the ridge. The Church Stretton information centre specialises in literature on all aspects of the Long Mynd and neighbouring hills.

The terrain is not unlike Dartmoor, and it can be hazardous when mists descend. Lengthy walks should not be attempted in snow or poor visibility, and driving can also be dangerous when vision is restricted. (See also Carding Mill Valley, above, and Rectory Wood, page 40.)

Oswestry Old Racecourse (OS 126: SJ 257310)

This open space, 2 miles (3 km) west of Oswestry on the B4580, was last used as a racecourse in the mid nineteenth century, and it has become a popular area for picnicking and walking. It lies on a high ridge with Offa's Dyke close by, and there are spectacular views of mid Wales on one side and the Shropshire plain on the other. It is possible to follow the Offa's Dyke Path southwards through attractive woodland.

The Stiperstones

The Stones are a remarkable series of quartzite outcrops, rising to a height of 1700 feet (520 metres) at the Devil's Chair. As this name implies, the area has always had a supernatural reputation. It is a bleak place, and the deserted lead mines at nearby Snailbeach (see page 88) and Shelve contribute to the eerie atmosphere. The Stiperstones are approximately 20 miles (32 km) south-

Carding Mill Valley, near Church Stretton.

west of Shrewsbury and are under the control of the Nature Conservancy Council. Easiest access is by way of the lane to Shelve, turning off the A488 at SJ 327997 (OS 137). About 5 miles (8 km) along the lane is a parking space at SJ 370977. The area must then be approached on foot along the lane to the north.

Wenlock Edge

This famous Shropshire hill feature is a steep escarpment running for 15 miles (24 km) between Much Wenlock and Craven Arms. It is seen at its best when approached from the north-west, where it appears as a dramatic tree-covered ridge. For centuries it has been quarried for the building stone that gives a distinctive appearance to Much Wenlock and surrounding villages. The B4371 passes along the ridge for a few miles and there is a fine viewpoint (OS 137: SO 575967) about a mile west of Presthope (but caution is necessary — it is a sheer, unfenced drop). Further exploration is possible at the Plough Inn (SO 570963). A long walk begins at SO 559953, leaving the main road and continuing along the escarpment past Wilder-hope Manor (see page 75). Visitors will find that the area behind the Edge — Hope Dale and Corvedale — is one of the least spoilt in Shropshire.

Whitecliffe (OS 137: SO 505743)

By leaving Ludlow by way of Ludford Bridge and then turning immediately right you can reach this extensive area of common land. After a few hundred yards a field on the right provides a famous view of Ludlow. A mile further on forest tracks provide good walking.

The Wrekin (OS 127: SJ 629083)

No visit to Shropshire is complete without a walk to the top of this hill. It is privately owned, but there are well defined public paths. It is easiest to reach it by way of a road that branches off the A5 west of Wellington at the junction that marks the end of the M54. This leads to Forest Glen (OS 127: SJ 638093), where it is possible to park and take the path that leads up the ridge to the summit. If preferred, the return can be made by continuing down the western end of the hill and walking back along the bottom on the northern side. (See page 50 for the hillfort.)

Lilleshall Abbey .

(Opposite) The view from Wenlock Edge.

4
Archaeological sites

Shropshire has few notable pre-iron age sites, although two important tracks used before the bronze age have been identified. One, the Port Way, is still used to cross the Long Mynd, while the other has been 'reconstructed' as a ridgeway running through south Shropshire from mid Wales to the Severn at Bewdley. One bronze age stone circle remains open to view; one or two others are too insignificant to be of interest to anyone but the specialist. The bronze age cemetery at Bromfield consists of little more than a few hummocks.

The county does, however, contain some of Britain's most spectacular iron age hillforts. Those included here are major sites that will provide a good walk, but the list is not complete and a study of the Ordnance Survey map will reveal many more. The Roman town of *Viroconium* is a site of immense potential — the excavated area is only a fraction of what has been revealed by aerial survey — but it will be many years before we know everything about this town that was built by Roman engineers for a native tribe to occupy.

Shropshire is fortunate in having several fine lengths of Offa's Dyke that can be easily walked.

The Berth (OS 126: SJ 429236)

This insignificant-looking site, 1½ miles (2.4 km) north of Baschurch, is included because of the mystery that surrounds it. It consists of two banks joined by a causeway, and its modest height (apparently useless for defence purposes) is probably explained by the fact that it once stood amid marshland that would have given adequate protection. Excavation has produced a sixth-century bronze cauldron, which indicates a settlement of some status. It has been strongly argued that this was the location of the legendary Pengwern, headquarters of Cynddylan, a Welsh chieftain who became overlord of the Cornovii for a time after the Roman departure. There is some evidence that he was buried at Baschurch in the seventh century. The site is on farmland and there is no public access without permission, although it can be seen at points along the triangle of roads that surround it.

Bromfield cemetery

Four bronze age barrows lie on Ludlow Racecourse at OS 137: SO 496776 and there is a fifth at SO 490779. Victorian excavation revealed signs of cremation and a bronze knife was recovered. Both sites lie beside roads.

Bury Ditches (OS 137: SO 327837)

This iron age fort, near Bishop's Castle, is small, about 7 acres (2.8 hectares), but has elaborate fortifications, improved in several recognisable stages and incorporating two carefully constructed entrances. The site is now covered by trees. The nearest parking point for cars is at SO 334840, where a short path leads to the fort. An alternative path from the western side begins at Guilden Down (SO 310827).

Caer Caradoc (Church Stretton) (OS 137: SO 477954)

This iron age fort is dramatically situated on the top of Shropshire's most spectacular peak. The path to it starts near the traffic lights on the A49 at Church Stretton and is easily discernible on the Ordnance Survey map. The going is wet in places. A notable feature of the settlement is the use of several outcrops of rock to reinforce the defences,

The lonely Mitchell's Fold stone circle near Chirbury.

especially at the southern end, where there was a vulnerable entrance. At the summit is a levelled platform with a waterhole just below it to the north. The fort was probably occupied by the Cornovii as a permanent settlement.

Caer Caradoc (Clun Forest) (OS 137: SO 310758)

The iron age fort stands isolated in deserted countryside at a height of over 1200 feet (365 metres), with fine views to the north. It is a small site of less than 3 acres (1.2 hectares), with a two-bank defence and extra fortification on the north side. There are two entrances. Access is possible from Chapel Lawn (SO 317764) but the easier route is probably the track starting at SO 304763.

Caynham Camp (OS 137: SO 545736)

The camp is an 8 acre (3.2 hectare) enclosure with rectangular ramparts, dating from the iron age. Excavation has revealed four phases of occupation, with modifications to the defences each time. Traces of timber buildings and grain storage pits have been found. There is access by various footpaths; the shortest is from the minor road at SO 536738 and another starts at a stile in Caynham churchyard.

Mitchell's Fold stone circle (OS 137: SO 304983)

Reached by taking the Priest Weston road out of Chirbury, this bronze age stone circle is 75 feet (23 metres) in diameter and has fifteen surviving uprights, although most of them are stumps. Its purpose is not known, but it was probably of religious or astronomical significance. The site and surrounding walks are exhilarating, and the views to the west are splendid. Access is by a potholed track leaving the minor road at SO 303977.

Nordy Bank (OS 137: SO 576847)

This is a small iron age fort of about 4 acres (1.6 hectares) on Brown Clee Hill. The defence works are minimal, but it is very accessible and makes a pleasant short walk. Park by the roadside at SO 573850 and the rounded hill is clearly visible.

Norton Camp (OS 137: SO 447820)

The iron age camp is to the south-east of Craven Arms, but access is extremely difficult. It stands at about 1000 feet (300 metres) and is 10 acres (4 hectares) in extent, surrounded by well defined banks and ditches. The site is now surrounded by trees but must have been chosen to command the valley of the river Onny below. Stokesay Castle (see

Wenlock Priory.

page 53) is a short distance to the west.

Offa's Dyke

Scholars argue about the purpose of this series of earthworks forming a line that stretches from Prestatyn on the North Wales coast to Chepstow in the south. The work was ordered by King Offa of Mercia in the late eighth century and consists mainly of a high bank with a ditch on the Welsh side. The original assumption that it was primarily a fortification has now been largely discarded, although it could have been manned in short lengths when required. One suggestion is that it was designed to assist in the control of cross-border trade; another view is that it was simply a definitive way of establishing the border between the kingdom of Mercia and Wales, perhaps negotiated rather than imposed by Offa.

Shropshire has some fine stretches of surviving dyke, and in most cases the long-distance footpath (see page 38) follows it closely.

Recommended lengths are: from the Ceiriog Valley to Carreg-y-Byg Farm (OS 126: SJ 264375 to SJ 253324); from the Old Racecourse, Oswestry, to Llanforda (OS 126: SJ 257310 to SJ 256283); west of Chirbury (OS 137: SO 233988 to SO 246947); west of Clun (OS 137: SO 258898 to SO 256827); south from Lower Spoad (OS 137: SO 257820 to SO 267763).

Old Oswestry (OS 126: SJ 296310)

This is the outstanding iron age settlement of the Welsh border and is easily accessible from Oswestry town centre by way of the Woodside estate. It is not much more than 100 feet (30 metres) high, but this was sufficient to command excellent views of the low-lying ground on three sides. The inner enclosure of 15 acres (6.0 hectares) is set within extensive and formidable banks and ditches, which show at least four phases of development. The well defined western entrance has a line of pits on each side, the purpose of which has not been discovered. The fort was evidently reoccupied after the departure of the Romans, and the eighth-century Wat's Dyke (see page 50) was aligned to include it.

Titterstone Clee (OS 137: SO 592779)

This was a very large iron age camp at the top of one of Shropshire's highest hills, but it has been disturbed by quarrying in modern times and it is now occupied by a radar establishment. It is accessible to the public, however, and although there is little to be seen of the hillfort it is well worth a visit for its superb position and views (see page 88 for industrial remains). The summit can almost be reached by car, turning off from the A4117 at SO 579757.

Viroconium Roman City and Museum, Wroxeter, Shrewsbury SY5 6PH (OS 126: SJ 565086). Telephone: 0743 761330. English Heritage.

Site open daily, but closed on Mondays from October to March and on Christmas Day, Boxing Day and New Year's Day. Museum open daily Easter to end of September; restricted winter opening.

The site is at the village of Wroxeter, beside the B4380. It is one of Britain's major Roman sites, although only a small part of the estimated 180 acres (72 hectares) covered by the town has yet been excavated. It was the first Roman town to be established on the Welsh border and eventually became the fourth largest in Britain. Started as a military fortress during the campaign against the Welsh in about AD 50, it was developed as a civilian town for the benefit of the local Cornovii tribe when the army was moved to Chester in AD 90.

Building progress was slow at first but accelerated after a visit by Hadrian, and the new forum was finished in AD 130 (the inscription stone, with a dedication to Hadrian, has been recovered). Archaeologists have traced at least two disasters following the handover to the Cornovii — a serious fire and the collapse of the forum façade. After the departure of the Romans the town evidently declined, but the site was reoccupied in the fifth century and extensive timber buildings were erected.

The visible remains include the large bath-house complex, with a massive section of wall containing the entrance. It is the largest surviving piece of Roman civil engineering yet discovered in Britain. On the other side of

The excavated bath-house complex at Viroconium.

the minor road to Wroxeter are the bases of the columns that made up the forum portico. Stone from the ruins was used for several local buildings, notably the churches at Atcham and Wroxeter: the latter has a gateway flanked by two Roman pillars.

Guidebooks are available at the site, and the small museum tells the story of *Viroconium* and its excavation and displays many of the smaller items found. The larger and more important items are on show in Rowley's House Museum at Shrewsbury (see page 83).

Wat's Dyke

Nothing is known for certain about the purpose of this earthwork, which can be traced sporadically from the Dee estuary to a point south of Oswestry. It predates Offa's Dyke and was possibly the work of the Mercian king Aethelbold (AD 716-57). It can be seen at Old Oswestry hillfort, and a substantial length flanks Oswestry cattle market on its western side.

The Wrekin (OS 127: SJ 629083)

The Wrekin is a dramatic hill, rising sharply and commanding extensive views to the north, west and south. It was an obvious site for a major hillfort and was probably the headquarters of the Cornovii tribe before the Romans moved them to nearby *Viroconium* (see page 49). Excavation has shown evidence of timber palisading, hut circles and drainage works, and also some indications of bronze age activity. The easiest way to the top starts at Forest Glen (SJ 638093), where it is possible to park and take a well-defined track up the ridge.

5
Castles and monastic buildings

Castles

For a county that has seen so much warfare Shropshire has surprisingly few extensive castle remains. A glance at the Ordnance Survey map will show that the western half of the county is sprinkled with 'mottes', but these were often little more than low mounds with a timber palisade, designed for short-term use during the innumerable local conflicts that occurred in the border area. The larger castles that have since almost disappeared, like those at Oswestry, Ellesmere and Bridgnorth, were allowed to disintegrate because they had outlived their military purpose and were unsuitable for alternative use, except possibly as a convenient source of stone for other building.

Among those that survived, Stokesay and Acton Burnell were always primarily country houses, while Shrewsbury Castle was the only military installation to be converted to domestic purposes in comparatively modern times. Ludlow has the finest example of a large castle site, largely owing to the grandiose ambitions of the Mortimer family and the fact that it was adapted in the post-medieval period as an administrative centre.

Acton Burnell Castle, Acton Burnell, Shrewsbury. English Heritage.
Open at all reasonable times.

The village of Acton Burnell is idyllically situated 6 miles (10 km) west of Much Wenlock, and its castle was never intended for any serious military purpose. Robert Burnell was Bishop of Bath and Wells between 1275 and 1292 but was also politically influential as Chancellor to Edward I. He was a major landowner in various parts of England, and the Shropshire estate was acquired mainly for the benefit of his younger relatives. Begun around 1283 (the licence to crenellate was granted in 1284), it qualifies as a castle mainly by having a tower at each corner of the rectangular structure. Like Stokesay, it was a fortified domestic residence rather than a military fortress. In the same year Edward I held a parliament at Acton Burnell, not in the castle but in a building nearby. In an adjacent field can be seen the end gables of a very long building; by tradition it is called the 'parliamentary barn', although there is no evidence that it was the site of the deliberations. The castle is now in the care of English Heritage. The remains are substantial, although the flooring has been lost and large gaps have been left in the walls following its use as a barn.

Bridgnorth Castle, Bridgnorth. Telephone enquiries: 0746 762231.
Open during daylight hours.

The castle site is behind St Mary's church. It has been turned into a small park, from which the visitor can get a vivid impression of the commanding position, but the surviving masonry is notable only for the big section of keep leaning at an acute angle.

Clun Castle, Clun, Craven Arms.
Open at all times.

This Norman stronghold of the Fitzalan family was built below and at some distance from the church in order to take advantage of a loop in the river Clun. On the side away from the river enormous earthworks were raised, and these are perhaps the most impressive feature of the site today. Apart from some small fragments, the remains comprise the shell of a formidable keep, built against the side of the motte rather than on top of it. The suggested reason for this unusual arrangement is that the motte was originally designed to take a light timber structure and the new stone keep was considered too heavy for the earth base. The keep is in a dangerous condition; it can be looked into from the top of the motte but not entered, but the extensive

Acton Burnell Castle, with the end wall of the 'parliamentary barn' nearby.

site is freely accessible and worth walking over.

Ludlow Castle, Ludlow. Telephone: 0584 873947.
Open daily except during December and January.

Ludlow has Shropshire's biggest and most complex set of castle buildings, spanning several centuries. Started by Roger de Lacy in the eleventh century, the castle was continually expanded and elaborated, especially after its acquisition by the powerful Mortimer family in 1307. After Edward IV became king in 1461 it became a royal outpost and later saw some famous guests, including the 'Princes in the Tower', Catherine of Aragon and Mary Tudor.

The entrance is in Castle Square in the centre of the town, and it leads into a large outer bailey with porter's lodge, prison and stables to the left. Access to the inner bailey containing the important buildings is by way of a bridge over a dry moat. The most impressive structure here is de Lacy's original keep, a striking contrast to the Elizabethan gateway. There is a good view of the whole castle from the first floor. The other eye-catching feature is the round nave of the Nor-man chapel, with some fine decoration. Against the northern boundary of the bailey is a range of much later buildings more appropriate to a palace than a castle. The most famous is the Great Hall, where the first performance of Milton's *Comus* was staged. On each side of it are state apartments, and the range also includes a garderobe tower and the Tudor lodgings. The inner bailey is the setting for an annual Shakespearian production as part of the Ludlow Festival.

Moreton Corbet Castle, Moreton Corbet, Shrewsbury SY4 4DW. English Heritage.

The village of Moreton Corbet is about 5 miles (8 km) south-east of Wem and 1$\frac{1}{2}$ miles (2.4 km) north of Shawbury. The ruins of its castle are of great interest in being a fusion of two structures, one of which is of a style unique in Shropshire. The unremarkable remains of an early castle are overshadowed by the shell of an ambitious mansion in stone-faced brick, apparently begun in the early sixteenth century and continued sporadically during the next 120 years. The large windows are the usual Elizabethan kind, but the face of the house has unusually florid decoration, with pilasters, cornices and ogee-shaped parapets. Robert Corbet, who initiated the building, had a strong interest in architecture and is reputed to have brought the design back with him after a journey to Italy.

The building was never completed, probably because of the impoverishment during the Civil War of Sir Vincent Corbet. It was garrisoned by Royalist forces and duly besieged, and the resulting damage, together with a fire and steady decay, has left a most unusual and evocative ruin.

Shrewsbury Castle, Castle Gates, Shrewsbury. Telephone: 0743 358516.
Grounds open daily, but closed Sundays from October to Easter. The building is closed temporarily following a terrorist bombing in 1992.

At Shrewsbury a remarkable meander of the Severn produces an area of land shaped like a sack with a narrow 'mouth' a few hundred yards wide. The river forms a natural moat, and the narrow strip of dry land was the obvious site for a castle from very early times. There was a Saxon fortification here, but the oldest sections of the present castle, the perimeter walls and gateway, date from the mid eleventh century. Roger de Montgomery completed the work in 1083. It was

rebuilt by Edward I between 1280 and 1300, and the Great Hall is basically of this period; the castle's main use at this time was as a base for Edward's incursions into Wales.

When the border conflicts petered out the castle was virtually abandoned, but it had to be hastily refortified at the outbreak of the Civil War in 1642, when it became a Royalist stronghold. It saw its last action in 1644, being captured by a Parliamentary force. Twenty years after the Restoration it was granted to Lord Newport as a residence, and in the late eighteenth century Thomas Telford completely remodelled it, producing the very unmilitary building that the visitor sees today. The castle houses the Shropshire Regimental Museum, opened in 1985 (page 84).

Stokesay Castle, Stokesay, Craven Arms SY7 9AH. Telephone: 0588 2544. English Heritage.
Open daily, except Tuesdays, from March to end of October, weekends in November.

Though actually a crenellated manor house, Stokesay is the most attractive of Shropshire's fortified buildings. Together with Stokesay church, it stands off the A49, a mile south of Craven Arms. It was last inhabited in 1728, and afterwards it deteriorated into service as a

Ludlow Castle.

Moreton Corbet Castle.

barn until rescued by the Allcroft family in the mid nineteenth century. Its remarkable restoration has been a matter of devoted private enterprise.

Building was begun in about 1240 by the de Say family of Clun, who established the north tower, but it was a Ludlow wool merchant, Lawrence de Ludlow, who extended it to include a great hall and residential quarters to the south. He obtained a licence to crenellate in 1291 and constructed the separate south tower for his garrison and a substantial curtain wall, which was demolished during the Civil War.

The castle is entered today by way of an exuberant but incongruous Elizabethan gateway (still inhabited), and on the other side of a small courtyard is the magnificent hall, lit by unusually large windows. The outstanding features here are the roof timbers and the thirteenth-century stairway leading to a retiring room, which has projecting diamond-paned windows. On the south side of the hall is a handsome solar — a drawing room embellished in the seventeenth century with wall panelling and an elaborate fireplace and over-

mantel. An outside staircase gives access to the bleak, functional south tower, on three storeys with stairs built within the walls.

The castle is unfurnished but fully roofed and well preserved.

The nearby church of St John the Baptist is described on page 64.

Whittington Castle, Whittington, Oswestry. *Open all year.*

Not much remains of this thirteenth-century castle built by the Fitzwarine family 2 miles (3 km) to the east of Oswestry. The present remains are unusual in being at ground level and the vanished motte was never more than 30 feet (9 metres) high, because it was adequately protected by surrounding marshland, which has since been drained. The outstanding features are the wide moat (still watered) and the impressive gatehouse with its twin drum towers. The small timber-framed house stands on the inner side of the gate.

Access is free. The landscaped site is a popular picnic stop for motorists on the A5 and there are tea rooms nearby.

Monastic buildings

Shropshire is known to have had thirteen religious houses. Only one was a nunnery — St Leonard's Priory (or White Ladies), near Shifnal. Four of the major monasteries were established for Augustinian canons, who were technically not monks but clergy observing monastic discipline. Their communities were at Lilleshall, Haughmond, Chirbury and Wombridge, and they were characterised by small numbers and isolated situations, circumstances that seem to have led to frequent lapses from monastic ideals.

The houses at Shrewsbury, Buildwas, Much Wenlock and Alberbury followed the Benedictine rule, although only Shrewsbury Abbey was independent. Buildwas was founded as one of a federation of houses subordinate to Savigny in Normandy and later became an outpost of the Cistercian order. Much Wenlock, with a history going back to the seventh century, became affiliated to the abbey of Cluny in Burgundy, while Alberbury was a rare example of a dependency of Grandmont in Limousin.

The local picture is complicated by the habit of setting up small cells of monks (often only two or three in number) in the area surrounding the main houses; indeed the communities whose ruins seem so large and magnificent normally housed quite small numbers. None of them appears to have led an untroubled existence.

Surviving records reveal periodic outbreaks of indiscipline, maladministration and even serious crime, and it would appear that Henry VIII's dissolution was in most cases a merciful end to a story of steady decline.

Most of the surviving traces of Shrewsbury Abbey were destroyed when Thomas Telford drove his Holyhead Road through them in 1834, leaving only the refectory pulpit isolated on one side (see page 29 for the Abbey Church). Remains at Wombridge and Alberbury are now negligible, and almost the only legacy of the priory at Chirbury is the unusually large parish church (see page 59). Virtually nothing remains of the monasteries at Morville, Bromfield (page 59), Preen and Ratlinghope. There are substantial ruins at the following sites, all of which are in the care of English Heritage.

The Norman nave at Buildwas Abbey.

The entrance to the chapter house at Haughmond Abbey.

Buildwas Abbey, Buildwas, Telford. English Heritage.
Open daily, but closed Mondays from October to March and Christmas and New Year holidays.
The ruins, off the B4380 west of Ironbridge, are not extensive, but what remains is superb. The abbey was founded in 1135 as a daughter house of Furness Abbey in Cumbria. The surviving buildings are of early date, about 1200, and the outstanding feature is the church nave with its magnificent arcades and east window openings. The other fine survival is the chapter house, which has columns supporting an elaborate vaulted roof. Here, and in an area to the north of the church, some interesting medieval tiles have been preserved.

Haughmond Abbey, Shrewsbury. English Heritage.
Open daily, but closed Mondays from October to March and Christmas and New Year holidays.
The abbey ruins are off the B5062 northeast of Shrewsbury. The first thing one sees on entering is an elegant bow window, unusual in an abbey and explained by the fact

that after the Dissolution the abbot's lodging became a private house. (It was altered in the seventeenth century and eventually burned down during the Civil War.) The original Augustinian foundation was established in 1135 by the Fitzalan family, but much rebuilding went on as the abbey prospered, and the oldest portions to be seen date from the late twelfth and early thirteenth centuries. What appears to be the nave of a church is the Great Hall: only the foundations of the church remain to the extreme north of the site. Particularly interesting are the entrance to the chapter house and the south-west doorway of the church, both elaborately carved and bearing statues of saints. Note also the latrine drainage system.

Lilleshall Abbey, Lilleshall, Newport. English Heritage.
Open at all times.
The village is off the A518 between Telford and Newport, and the abbey is about a mile to the south-east. As at Buildwas, the most impressive remains are those of the church, which was about 230 feet (70 metres) long, and there is a fine vista through the west doorway. The building dates from the mid

twelfth century, and this doorway is a good example of the carving and moulding of the period. The interior shows signs of later embellishment; little remains of what must have been an elaborate east window, but there is a fine window in the north wall. The most celebrated feature at Lilleshall is the doorway from the nave into the cloister, multi-shafted and beautifully carved in unusual designs, and there are several other good door arches in the former cloister area. Unfortunately the chapter house is now roofless.

Wenlock Priory, Much Wenlock. English Heritage.
Open daily, but closed Mondays from October to March and Christmas and New Year holidays.

The ruins of the priory lie within easy walking distance of the town centre. They indicate a site of impressive size, and the church alone must have been of cathedral-like proportions. The original foundation was established in the late seventh century by the Mercian king Merewalh for his daughter Milburga, who inspired several legends during her lifetime. It appears to have fallen into ruins two hundred years later (the theory that it was de-stroyed by the Danes is now largely discounted) but a new house was built by Leofric of Mercia on the same site. Roger de Montgomery was responsible for starting the present buildings soon after the Norman Conquest, and St Milburga's body, 'sound and uncorrupted', is reputed to have been discovered during the new work.

After the Dissolution the prior's lodging became a private house and remains as such today. The ruins of the church give an impression of its former magnificence, with the south transept rising to a height of 70 feet (21 metres) and incorporating a wealth of architectural detail. The adjacent chapter house is notable not only for the customary decoration on its three-arched entrance but also for the complex pattern of intersecting arches on its wall. Two panels of the well-head in the monks' lavatorium are very imaginatively carved.

White Ladies Priory, near Shifnal. English Heritage.
About 2 miles (3 km) north-east of Tong, ruins survive of the small twelfth-century church of Shropshire's only nunnery, the Priory of St Leonard.

6
Churches and chapels

The Shropshire towns have some magnificent ecclesiastical buildings, but there are also villages and hamlets with churches that are remarkable for their architecture, historical associations or simply their individuality. The town churches are described in chapter 2 and this chapter concentrates on those not-to-be-missed churches that could nevertheless be overlooked by the visitor because they are remote or are situated in places that are otherwise unremarkable. Although this list is reasonably comprehensive, there are other churches that would repay a visit.

Acton Burnell: St Mary. 7 miles (11 km) south-east of Shrewsbury.

St Mary's is one of the most complete thirteenth-century village churches in Britain, renowned for the memorials in the north transept. Shropshire is not rich in good memorial brasses, and the one here is probably the best of them. The tomb is that of Sir Nicholas Burnell, who died in 1382, and it portrays him in a complete suit of armour of the period. Even more impressive is the table monument with carved effigies of Richard Lee and his wife (1591). The wall memorial of 1632 to Sir Humphrey Lee was worked by Nicholas Stone, who was master mason to Charles I.

Alberbury: St Michael and All Angels. See page 11.

Aston Eyre. 4 miles (6.5 km) west of Bridgnorth on the B4368.

The church is Norman and noted for a particularly fine carved tympanum, portraying Christ's entry into Jerusalem. It is probably by a member of the Herefordshire School, whose work is better known in churches like Kilpeck.

Atcham: St Eata. 4 miles (6 km) south-east of Shrewsbury on the A5.

The church of St Eata, the only one in Britain with this dedication, stands in an attractive situation beside the Severn. There is a Saxon window in the north wall, which contains stones from the Roman city of *Viroconium* nearby (see page 49). The tiny sanctuary is strangely at odds with the large

chancel fitted out with stalls for a vast choir. The medieval east window in delicate browns and golds was brought from Bacton in Herefordshire, and there is Elizabethan glass in a north window commemorating a lady-in-waiting to Elizabeth I. The carvings on the priest's stall date from the sixteenth century as does a memorial tablet in incised alabaster by the pulpit. Few churches in Shropshire have survived restoration so well.

Barrow: St Giles. 3 miles (5 km) east of Much Wenlock off the B4376.

Reached by way of a narrow lane almost opposite the school, the church of St Giles is usually locked, but the key can be obtained from the house opposite. The plain Norman tower and rubble stonework look unremarkable, but a walk round to the little chancel will reveal the irregular blocks of masonry and a double-splayed window that indicate Saxon origins.

It has been reliably established that the present chancel was an eleventh-century rebuild (probably to about the same size) of an earlier chapel established by Wenlock Priory. This makes it one of the most important pieces of late Saxon work to have survived in the county. It is divided from the nave by a flattened Saxon arch, and a puzzling feature on the south side is a very early doorway crudely inserted by cutting into a window space. The nave is a little later, and its west doorway has a naively carved tympanum on the tower side — it was evidently the original entrance, left in place when the twelfth-century tower was built.

Some charming monuments in the nave commemorate servants of the local Forester family of Willey Hall, and in the churchyard is the grave of Tom Moody, a famous Forester huntsman.

Battlefield: St Mary Magdalene. On the extreme northern outskirts of Shrewsbury off the A49.

In 1403 Henry IV led his army into battle here against a motley group of rebels led by the Earl of Northumberland and his son Harry Hotspur. As a thanksgiving for his victory the king ordered the building of this collegiate church and endowed a college of priests to serve it. There is a small nave, but the chancel is the focal point; it is broad and uncluttered with almost no colour. Decoration takes the form of carved representations of knights, and the roof beams carry the coats of arms of the kings' followers. Despite much restoration, the church retains its atmosphere of cold medieval austerity. A pavement of encaustic tiles was laid in the nineteenth century.

Benthall: St Bartholomew. 4 miles (6 km) north-east of Much Wenlock on the B4375.

St Bartholomew's church lies in the shadow of Benthall Hall (see page 67), but it can be visited independently of the house. From the outside it is something of a hotch-potch of styles, having been altered at various times since the original nave and chancel were built in 1667 to replace a building damaged in a Civil War skirmish. The additions include a tall tower, a Gothic vestry and an apse-like extension at the west end, built to provide easier access to the gallery.

The interior owes much to the eighteenth century, with its box pews, pretty miniature organ and the pulpit and reader's desk on each side of the chancel arch. (Unfortunately the original three-decker pulpit was removed in 1892.) Typical also of the time is the plaster ceiling which partly hides a hammer-beam roof. Two features dominate an otherwise plain church. One is a magnificent chancel monument, the tablet framed sumptuously in gold and surmounted by an open pediment with a coat of arms. The other is Edward Burra's startling portrayal of the Coronation of the Virgin, a large and exuberant modern painting.

Bettws-y-crwyn: St Mary. Off the B4368 7 miles (11 km) west of Clun. OS 137: SO 206814.

This remote little church, 1700 feet (520 metres) up in the Clun Forest, is well worth the steep drive from the main road. There is no real village here, and the names on the sides of the pews are of farms that provided the congregation. The church was neatly restored in the nineteenth century, but two outstanding features remain: a carved rood screen of great delicacy and a set of roof timbers, massive but elegantly patterned, which are probably the finest in any small church in the county. From the churchyard there is a panoramic view to the east.

Bromfield: St Mary. On the A49 3 miles (5 km) north-west of Ludlow.

Bromfield was once the site of a Benedictine priory, and the fine gatehouse survives close to the church. St Mary's has some traces of the original foundation, but it is noted now for its eccentric interior. In 1672 the chancel was decorated with paintings in an amateurish way. Only the ceiling remains now, but it is enough to indicate the dubious taste of the enterprise. The devotional representations tend to be dominated by obese cherubs draped in texts. The Victorian triptych behind the altar is another exotic feature. Note the memorial at the back of the church to Henry Hickman, for long an unacknowledged pioneer of anaesthetics.

Chirbury: St Michael. On the A490 3½ miles (6 km) north-east of Montgomery.

St Michael's church is unusually large for a village of modest size like Chirbury. The reason is that the church was originally part of an Augustinian priory and acted as the mother church for chapels scattered over a wide area. The medieval nave with leaning pillars is wide and very high and must have been even bigger before part of it was turned into a chancel in the nineteenth century. The Victorians splendidly refurbished the chancel and sanctuary, notably with a striking mosaic reredos. A curious Elizabethan *memento mori* was left on one wall of the chancel. The church's most treasured possession is a medieval mould used to make figures of the Virgin and Child for pilgrims to a local well. The timber-framed school house stands behind the church.

Church Stretton: St Laurence. See page 14.

Claverley: All Saints. 6 miles (10 km) east of Bridgnorth.

All Saints is a most exciting church. When it received sympathetic restoration in 1902 the limewash was scraped off the interior walls to reveal extensive medieval wall painting. One large frieze on the north arcade shows knights in combat and is reminiscent of the Bayeux Tapestry. It has been dated as early as 1200 and was apparently overpainted in the fifteenth century, together with the chancel arch, which shows traces of a large representation of the Last Judgement.

The church reveals several architectural styles, with a Norman north arcade, a later south aisle and two early Elizabethan chapels flanking the chancel. Both were built for the local Gatacre family and there are two fine incised alabaster memorials to them on the south side. Here also is an altar tomb with delicately carved effigies of Sir Robert Broke, who died in 1558, and his two wives. An even older memorial (1448) has been mounted

on the nave wall at the entrance to the north chapel. The church has two notable fonts; the one in use is probably early Norman, while the other is considerably older.

Cleobury Mortimer: St Mary. See page 15.

Clun: St George. See page 16.

Condover: St Mary and St Andrew. 4 miles (6 km) south of Shrewsbury off the A49.

The church of St Mary and St Andrew stands within 100 yards (90 metres) of Condover Hall (see page 71) and is notable for containing a good deal of seventeenth-century work, a period not greatly represented in Shropshire.

From the churchyard gate it is possible to see three distinct building styles: a Norman north transept, the nave and tower of the 1660s and a strange porch of 1878. The interior, however, is unified by a spectacular hammerbeam roof spanning the wide nave — the finest of its kind in the county, and revealed only in 1878 when the plaster ceiling was removed. The chancel is entirely Victorian, and when it was built a north chapel was added to house monuments to the occupants of the hall. Some of these are very fine, particularly a flowing sculpture of 1746 by Roubiliac, a dramatic kneeling figure by George Frederick Watts and a poignant

Edgmond church.

memorial to the young Alice Cholmondeley, carved by her husband.

Diddlebury: St Peter. 6 miles (9.5 km) north-east of Craven Arms on the B4368.

The modern village of Diddlebury lies beside the road from Craven Arms to Much Wenlock, but the old village centre is half a mile (800 metres) off the road — an attractive place consisting of a few cottages, a farm, a school, a stream and St Peter's church on its elevated site. The west doorway into the tower is a modest affair in a simple late Norman style, but it obviously replaced a huge entrance, of which the flattened arch is still visible. Otherwise the exterior is featureless, but inside there is a striking expanse of herringbone masonry on the north wall of the nave, indicating a late Saxon or very early Norman origin. In the same wall a Saxon window survives, together with decorated fragments of a Saxon cross.

Eaton-under-Heywood: St Edith. 5^1/2 miles (9 km) south-east of Church Stretton. OS 137: SO 500900.

St Edith's church is tucked away under Wenlock Edge and almost engulfed by trees that spread down from the top. It long ago lost its village, and only a tiny group of buildings surrounds it now. It stands on a hill and the floor follows the natural slope up to the altar. The earliest parts of the building date from the twelfth century and the nave is early Norman, while the chancel and tower are probably a little older. The notable feature here is a fourteenth-century oak effigy, possibly of a lord of the manor, but there are also some superb structural woodwork and a striking pulpit with a canopy dated 1670. The nineteenth-century font cover, while hardly appropriate to the old and simple font itself, is a remarkable piece of carving by a local man.

Edgmond: St Peter. Off the B5062 3 miles (5 km) west of Newport.

Edgmond has developed as a dormitory village and the old collegiate church, with the Provost's house surviving from the original foundation, lies a long way from the centre. Not much of the original Norman work remains but the font is an eleventh-century

carved tub and one of the oldest in the county. The east window is a fine piece of work by the Victorian artist Kempe, and there is a large window at the west end with an appealing portrayal of St Francis. The church's main treasure, a fine Elizabethan brass memorial, is covered by a carpet, presumably as a defence against brass-rubbers. The exterior is full of character, with battlements, pinnacles and gargoyles.

Edstaston: St Mary the Virgin. 2^1/2 miles (4 km) north of Wem on the B5476.

This is regarded as one of Shropshire's finest Norman churches in regular use. Original features still remaining include the huge wooden doors and their ironwork, the masonry of the north and south walls and two finely arched entrances with elaborate carving. The walls are covered with traces of early medieval painting, some strikingly recognisable, and a pleasant survival of a later date is a set of lamps now converted to electricity.

Heath Chapel. OS 137: SO 557856.

The little chapel stands by itself in a field to the north-east of Bouldon and 3^1/2 miles (6 km) east of Diddlebury. Its shell has remained virtually unaltered since early Norman times. Apart from the carving on the door it is totally undecorated, and the interior contains box pews, a font and a minimum of other furniture. The key can be obtained from a nearby farm. In the field to the north are traces of the deserted village that the chapel once served.

Hodnet: St Luke. 6 miles (10 km) south-west of Market Drayton.

Hodnet is best known for the gardens of the Hall (see page 74) but the church should not be missed. It stands in a village that is large for Shropshire, full of mellow brick and timber framing, and the church is appropriately grand, with a distinctive octagonal tower. The oldest part of the building is the south aisle, virtually a nave in itself, and one can see the outlines of the original Norman door and windows on which later openings have been superimposed. The rich window in the east end of this aisle is by the Shropshire artist David Evans.

St Peter's, Melverley, is a rare example of a timber-framed church .

The main nave and chancel belong to the fourteenth century and are exceptionally large and finely proportioned. Another imposing east window dominates a sanctuary which has a flanking chapel built in 1870 for the Heber-Percys, owners of Hodnet Hall. The most famous member of the family was Bishop Heber, author of many familiar hymns, including 'Brightest and best are the sons of the morning' and 'From Greenland's icy mountains'. Other notable features here are the fine tiles paving both sanctuaries and the floor of the main chancel. At the back of the church are a font that looks Norman but is probably an imitation and a collection of chained books.

The size of the building and its wealth of superb craftsmanship from many centuries make it one of Shropshire's most impressive village churches.

Holdgate: Holy Trinity. 9 miles (14 km) south-west of Much Wenlock. OS 137: SO 562896.

In Norman times Holdgate was important enough to have a castle, parts of which are incorporated into a farmhouse, so Holy Trinity church is over-large for what has now become a tiny agricultural hamlet in

Corvedale, the sparsely populated valley that separates Wenlock Edge from the Clee Hills. The church is not beautiful to look at, but its porch conceals one of the finest Norman doorways in the county — a three-stepped arch, each step embellished with distinctive designs, and all contained within a hood mould with different patterns on its two halves.

The nave has a rough Norman austerity, but the font is a magnificent example of bold abstract carving, typical of the most superior craftsmanship of the twelfth century. The benches may well be of the sixteenth century, while the splendid Cresset family pew dates from a hundred years later, featuring shafts and an elaborate heraldic canopy. On the outside of the south chancel wall is an eroded Sheila-na-gig, a female fertility figure of which about half a dozen examples survive in Shropshire.

Hughley: St John the Baptist. 5 miles (8 km) south-west of Much Wenlock off the B4371.

Hughley has become famous for a mistake by A. E. Housman, who referred in a poem to 'Hughley steeple' while the church has only a modest belfry. However, it has a fine fifteenth-century chancel screen, a rarity in Shropshire. There are some medieval tiles behind it. The roof also dates from the fifteenth century. The church clock was apparently donated by the Earl of Bradford in recognition of a win by his horse in the 1892 Derby.

Langley Chapel. 1¼ miles (2 km) south of Acton Burnell. English Heritage.

As the population it served had dispersed long before the nineteenth century, the chapel, now in state care, was not subjected to Victorian restoration and is a fine example of a church fitted out in seventeenth-century puritan style. The chapel is normally open during daylight hours.

Little Stretton: All Saints. 2 miles (3 km) south-west of Church Stretton on the B4370.

This church is included because it comes close to being a folly. Erected in 1903, it is in black and white timber-framed style and thatched. Set beside a trim lawn with flower beds, it could be mistaken for a country cottage. The interior is severe, with a lining of varnished pine boards, but there is a handsome chancel arch.

Llanyblodwel: St Michael. 6 miles (10 km) south-west of Oswestry on the A495.

The Reverend John Parker, a nineteenth-century incumbent, decided to redesign Llanyblodwel church to his own eccentric taste. A curious bullet-shaped tower and spire became the outstanding exterior feature, but the inside was transformed into a riot of colour, with painted texts, gilding and patterns on almost every available surface. Fortunately he retained the twelfth-century doorway, the chancel arch formed by structural timbers and a long chancel screen. It is a most unusual church in an idyllic riverside setting.

Ludlow: St Laurence. See page 20.

Melverley: St Peter. OS 126: SJ 333166.

The journey along narrow lanes to Melverley seems endless, but the reward is one of the county's most appealing churches. Standing a few feet from the river Vyrnwy, it is the only fifteenth-century timber-framed church in Shropshire open to the public. It was constructed by local labour in 1406 after Owain Glyndwr's men had destroyed the original building, and it has remained basically unaltered since. The tiny interior space is massively divided into two halves by a screen that is an essential part of the structure, and there is a minute gallery reached by ancient

The west front of the seventeenth-century church at Minsterley.

and perilous stairs. Amid the rough-hewn timber the Elizabethan altar and Jacobean pulpit look almost modern, but the most recent addition is the east window, installed as a war memorial. The crudely cut octagonal font is almost certainly pre-Norman.

Minsterley: Holy Trinity. 8 miles (13 km) south-west of Shrewsbury on the A488.

This is a very strange-looking building, a rare example of a seventeenth-century church. Built in red brick and elaborately buttressed, it has a highly embellished west front with diamond-pane windows, decorated stonework and intricate carving. All this is surmounted by an odd little belfry. Inside is a collection of 'maiden garlands' made of paper flowers and cloth and hung in the church after being carried in the funeral processions of unmarried girls.

Richards Castle: All Saints. At Batchcott, 4 miles (6.5 km) south of Ludlow on the B4361.

Richards Castle is in Herefordshire, but its church is in Shropshire — a mile (1.6 km) away near the hamlet of Batchcott. All Saints was completed in 1892, the work of the eminent architect Richard Norman Shaw, as a replacement for the dilapidated St Bartholomew's, which still stands beside Richards Castle about a mile to the west of the modern village.

The site is on gently rising ground that gives the church a commanding position when approached from the south. It is built in pale local stone that has yellowed slightly with age, and the style is Shaw's own version of fourteenth-century Gothic. A formal walk leads to a tower which is almost detached from the church and has something of the effect of a gatehouse. The interior is extremely austere — a huge space with high walls of near-white stone and a sweeping arcade dividing the nave from the south aisle. One of the few touches of colour is the huge triptych over the altar, and there is fine craft work in the stalls, pews, iron chancel screen and intricately carved pulpit. It must have seemed alarmingly modern, perhaps intimidating, to a country congregation used to a small medieval church.

Selattyn: St Mary. 3^1/$_2$ miles (6 km) north-west of Oswestry on the B4579.

The church of St Mary is unusual in being below road level, a situation that gives it a dramatic background of steep pasture-land. Unusual also for Shropshire are the red-tiled roof and the eighteenth-century three-decker tower. The interior is basically the result of Victorian restoration, during which the outstanding feature of the church was revealed and refurbished. It is a rare example of a carved barrel ceiling over the chancel, half-cylindrical in shape and composed of over two hundred small panels.

Also on display are three massive beams that once formed part of the rood screen.

Shifnal: St Andrew. See page 27.

Shrewsbury: St Chad. See page 30.

Shrewsbury Abbey: Holy Cross. See page 29.

Stanton Lacy: St Peter. 4^1/$_2$ miles (7 km) north-west of Ludlow off the B4365.

The first impression of St Peter's church is one of primitive strength. A short but massive tower divides nave from chancel and the west wall is like a cliff face. This, with the north wall and transept, is a striking example of Saxon work, probably of the mid eleventh century, incorporating characteristic pilasters. The chancel is long and low compared with the nave and is dominated by the lurid east window (all the stained glass is Victorian and by a Shrewsbury artist). It overshadows the charmingly painted reredos and the unusual altar front with its elegant modelling. Outside in the south wall are two recessed tombs with unidentifiable effigies worn almost smooth.

Stokesay: St John the Baptist. 1 mile (1.6 km) south-east of Craven Arms off the A49.

St John the Baptist's, which is the parish church of Craven Arms, lies almost within the grounds of Stokesay Castle (see page 53) and is notable for the substantial rebuilding that took place after damage during a Civil War skirmish in 1646. It is one of the few churches in England to have been restored

The church of St Mary Magdalene at Battlefield.

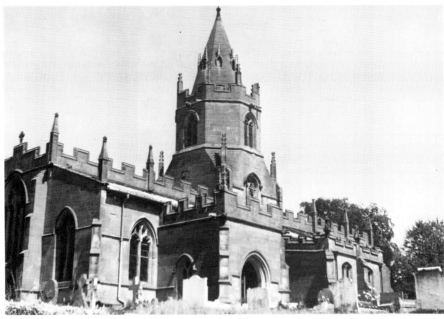

Tong church, the 'village Westminster Abbey'.

during Cromwell's regime. The south door-way is the only feature to have survived from the original Norman church. It leads into a nave that is dominated by giant texts that cover the walls — the Creed, the Commandments and a whole stretch of Exodus are laid out in huge, laborious script.

The box pews include two very substantial canopied versions for the gentry, and some rough late medieval benches survive under the gallery, a rather delicate eighteenth-century addition. The pulpit, with its reader's desk and sounding board, is a fine piece very much in keeping with the other nave fittings. Two distinctive stained glass windows commemorating Edward Hotchkiss, 'the first Shropshire aviator', and Ernest Tredinnick are of particular interest.

Stottesdon: St Mary. 6 miles (10 km) north of Cleobury Mortimer on minor roads off the B4363.

The church contains much of interest, including a tympanum that is probably pre-Norman. The richly carved font has been claimed as the finest of its kind in Shropshire.

Tong: St Mary the Virgin with St Bartholomew. 12 miles (19 km) south-east of Newport on the A41.

The church has acquired the title of 'the village Westminster Abbey' because of the number and scale of the monuments to the Vernon family, whose ancestor, Lady Elizabeth Pembruge, established the church as a collegiate foundation in 1410. The monuments, although striking, are obtrusive and out of scale with the building, with the exception of the early Tudor brass to Sir William Vernon and his wife. The small chantry — the 'Golden Chapel' — has a fine vaulted ceiling, elaborate exterior carving and an unusual wall bust of Sir Arthur Vernon. The long chancel is notable for its ancient stalls and a restored east window with much fifteenth-century glass. A curiosity in the porch is a Victorian noticeboard laying down rules for the celebratory ringing of the Great Bell.

Wem: St Peter and St Paul. See page 32.

Whitchurch: St Alkmund. See page 34.

7
Historic houses and gardens

Although Shropshire abounds in large houses and estates comparatively few have been opened to the public, and none has been commercialised in the Woburn or Longleat manner. Opening dates and times may be changed and it is advisable to check them before making a special journey.

Adcote, Little Ness, Shrewsbury SY4 2JY. Telephone: 0939 260202. 7 miles (11 km) north-west of Shrewsbury off the A5.
Now a school but open to the public by appointment during the summer months.

Adcote, a Grade I listed building, is a large Victorian country mansion designed in sixteenth-century 'baronial' style by Norman Shaw and built in 1879. The outstanding feature is the imposing hall, with minstrel's gallery, vast fireplace, bay window and a roof carried on stone arches. It is on an almost superhuman scale, but its clean-cut lines are devoid of vulgarity. There is little furniture on display, but the fine tiled fireplaces should be noted. The house, both inside and out, is a revelation to the layman who thinks he knows what is meant by 'Victorian architecture'.

Attingham Park, Atcham, Shrewsbury SY4 4TP. Telephone: 074377 203. 4 miles (6 km) south-east of Shrewsbury on the B4380 (formerly A5). National Trust.
House open Easter to September, afternoons Saturday to Wednesday. Grounds open daily throughout the year (except Christmas Day).

Attingham is one of the great eighteenth-century houses of Shropshire. It was designed in 1783 by George Steuart (architect of St Chad's church, Shrewsbury) in an unusual form; the central three-storey block containing the principal rooms is connected on each side to smaller 'pavilions' by means of colonnaded passages. The façade includes a very tall portico. Steuart's client was Noel Hill, first Lord Berwick, who originally had portions of an earlier house incorporated into the design, but these were later demolished.

There were early modifications in 1807 by John Nash, whose main contributions were a fine picture gallery with cast-iron window frames and a grand new staircase in a circular well. The grounds, which include a deer park, were landscaped by Humphry Repton. The interior decoration, especially the plasterwork, is superb, and there is a boudoir painted in the eighteenth-century French manner. Particular features are a display of Regency silver, some fine furniture (including a collection of Italian pieces) and the Italian and Dutch paintings in Nash's gallery. The grounds can be visited separately.

Benthall Hall, Broseley. Telephone: 0952 882159. 4 miles (6 km) north-east of Much Wenlock off the B4375. National Trust.
Open April to end of September, Wednesday and Sunday afternoons.

The home of Mr and Mrs James Benthall, this is a late sixteenth-century house with an additional wing dating from a later period, and the façade has an interesting array of gables, chimneys and bay windows. The main entrance door is notable for a representation of the five wounds of Christ, a feature believed to be the explanation of 'the symbols at your door' in the song 'Green Grow the Rushes'.

The interior has excellent panelling and plasterwork, and an outstanding carved oak staircase of the early seventeenth century. In a room off the library is a concealed hiding place characteristic of houses owned by Catholic families. The furniture includes some seventeenth-century pieces and the rooms are embellished with Caughley china.

Hawkstone Hall, Weston-under-Redcastle.

(Opposite) Shipton Hall.

Attingham Park, designed by George Steuart for the first Lord Berwick.

The garden, restored by Mr and Mrs Benthall, is a plantsman's delight. The seventeenth-century parish church nearby should not be missed (see page 59).

Boscobel House, Tong, Shifnal. Telephone: 0902 850244. 3¹/₂ miles (6 km) north-east of Tong, signposted off the A41. English Heritage.
Open daily, but closed on Mondays between 1st October and Easter.

It was at Boscobel House that Charles II took refuge after the battle of Worcester. There is an oak tree there reputed to have

Boscobel House, showing some of the later additions to the original structure.

The oak tree at Boscobel.

Burford House Gardens and Treasures Plant Centre, Burford, Tenbury Wells, Worcestershire WR15 8HQ. Telephone: 0584 810777.
Open all year, Mondays to Saturdays and Sunday afternoons.

Set on the Shropshire bank of the river Teme, Burford House Gardens comprise extensive lawns and a large collection of plants from all over the world built up by John Treasure since 1954, when he purchased the house and grounds. Throughout the year there are plants and planting combinations to interest all gardeners, and the retail plant centre of Treasures of Tenbury is situated near the entrance. The National Clematis Collection is held at the gardens, though not all of it is accessible to the public. Refreshments are available at the tea rooms.

grown from an acorn of the tree in which Charles hid. The house was built in about 1600 as a timber-framed hunting lodge, but there have been extensions and alterations since. The main features are two concealed rooms used by Charles when he was not hiding in the oak. An attractive interpretative display plots his escape route across England. The outbuildings contain a restaurant and a shop.

Condover Hall, Condover, Shrewsbury SY5 7AH. 4 miles (6 km) south of Shrewsbury, off the A49. Telephone: 0743 872320.
Open during August only, by appointment with Condover Hall school.

An outstanding Elizabethan mansion with eighteenth-century interior features, Condover Hall is used as a school for the blind. See page 60 for the nearby parish church.

Burford House Gardens.

The gatehouse at Stokesay Castle.

(Opposite) The Severn Valley Railway

The Orangery at Weston Park.

The Dorothy Clive Garden, Willough-bridge, Market Drayton TF9 4EU. Telephone: 0630 647237. On A51 6 miles (10 km) north-east of Market Drayton.
Open April to October, daily.
In addition to a wide range of specimen plants, including many rare varieties, the 7 acre (2.8 hectare) Dorothy Clive Garden features a quarry garden with a spectacular waterfall, a scree and water garden and pleasant woodland areas. There are exceptional views over the surrounding countryside.

Dudmaston, Quatt, Bridgnorth. Telephone: 0746 780866. 4 miles (6 km) south-east of Bridgnorth on the A442. National Trust.
Open April to end of September, Wednesday and Sunday afternoons.
The house is predominantly of the early eighteenth century, symmetrical, but solid rather than elegant. In addition to its well-proportioned rooms and fine furniture, the house contains pictures and sculpture, including works by Matisse, Nicholson, Barbara Hepworth and Henry Moore and a collection of watercolours and Dutch flower paintings that once belonged to the Darby family of Coalbrookdale. The attractive informal lakeside gardens include flowering shrubs and trees and a rockery, and there are woodlands.

Hawkstone Park. See under Weston-under-Redcastle, page 34.

Hodnet Hall Gardens, Hodnet, Market Drayton TF9 3NN. Telephone: 063084 202. 5½ miles (9 km) south-west of Market Drayton on the A53.
Open every afternoon from April to the end of September.
The hall, an Elizabethan-style mansion built in the 1870s, is not open, but visitors are admitted to the gardens, which are among the most famous in Britain. The late Brigadier A. G. W. Heber-Percy spent thirty years transforming a wilderness into the 60 landscaped acres (24 ha) on view today, making a particular feature of water from underground springs, which runs through a chain of lakes rich in wildlife. There are some splendid trees and a magnificent show of shrubs and flowers throughout the spring and summer. Gifts and plants may be purchased and teas are available in the seventeenth-century tea rooms with their big-game trophies.

Mawley Hall, Cleobury Mortimer, near Kidderminster, Worcestershire DY14 8PN. 2 miles (3 km) east of Cleobury Mortimer off the A4117.
Open on written application to the Adminis-

trator at the above address.

This is a mid eighteenth-century house, and the plain exterior conceals some outstanding interior decoration, including panelling, plasterwork, marquetry floors and a splendid staircase.

Morville Hall, Bridgnorth. 5 miles (8 km) south-east of Much Wenlock on the A458. *Open on written application to the National Trust tenant.*

The hall is basically sixteenth-century but with eighteenth-century additions. It has an immense façade comprising the house itself and two flanking lodges of substantial size. The attractive gardens adjacent to the hall have been restored by the tenants.

Shipton Hall, Much Wenlock TF13 6JZ. Telephone: 074636 225. 6 miles (10 km) south-west of Much Wenlock on the B4378. *Open Thursday afternoons only from Easter to end of September, also Bank Holiday Sundays and Mondays (except Christmas and New Year).*

The privately owned house occupies a commanding position beside the road behind its walled garden. It was built by Richard Lutwyche in the late sixteenth century and is a fine example of the local building stone. The façade is unusual in having a four-storey tower asymmetrically placed above the porch, reducing the severity of the building in an attractive way. The interior was extensively remodelled in the eighteenth century, resulting in a handsome hall, staircase and library. The architect, Thomas F. Pritchard, was also responsible for the stable block and other Georgian additions. Some original Tudor and later panelling has been preserved. Paintings and furniture are on display, but the notable feature is the collection of china. A medieval dovecote is behind the house, and the parish church is also situated in the grounds and may be reached via the garden.

Upton Cressett Hall, Bridgnorth. Telephone: 074631 307. 4 miles (6 km) west of Bridgnorth off the A458. *Open Thursday afternoons from May to September.*

The hall is a substantial timber-framed house with brick facing, mainly of the mid sixteenth century. There are signs of at least three stages of building, the earliest being a medieval great hall with fine timbers, and some varied examples of Elizabethan chimneys can be seen. The ground-floor rooms have good Jacobean furniture and there is a most interesting first-floor room that reveals the timbers of the great hall. The gatehouse of about 1580 is impressively turreted and gabled. The rooms here were intended to be lived in and have decorative plaster ceilings. The Norman church nearby is closed but the key can be obtained at the house.

Weston Park, Weston-under-Lizard, Shifnal TF11 8LE. Telephone: 0952 76207. 5 miles (8 km) north-east of Shifnal on the A5. *Open weekends and Bank Holidays from Easter to September, daily in Spring Bank Holiday week and during August, daily except Mondays and Fridays in June and July.*

Although it is just in Staffordshire, Weston Park is usually thought of as being in Shropshire. The fine mansion of the Restoration period was built by Lady Wilbraham in 1671 and for most of the time since then it has been the ancestral home of the Earls of Bradford. The magnificent art collection includes works by Holbein, Van Dyck, Gainsborough, Reynolds and Stubbs, and the furnishings include Gobelin and Aubusson tapestries. 'Capability' Brown landscaped the grounds in the eighteenth century, with three lakes and many trees. Now there are a herd of deer, rare breeds of sheep, nature trails, a miniature steam railway and a museum of country bygones.

Wilderhope Manor, Easthope, Much Wenlock. Telephone: 06943 353. 7 miles (11 km) south-west of Much Wenlock off the B4371. National Trust. *Open Wednesday and Saturday afternoons from April to September, Saturday afternoons only from October to March.*

Now used as a youth hostel, the manor is an isolated late sixteenth-century house with a frontage very similar to that at Shipton Hall. The notable features are an original spiral staircase and a series of exceptional plaster ceilings of the early seventeenth century.

Ironbridge Gorge Museum: Foundry Alley at Blists Hill.

(Opposite) Ironbridge Gorge Museum: The Museum of the River and Visitor Centre.

8
Museums and other places to visit

Acton Scott

Acton Scott Historic Working Farm, Wenlock Lodge, Acton Scott, Church Stretton SY6 6QN. Signposted off the A49 4 miles (6 km) south of Church Stretton. Telephone: 0694 781306 or 781307.

Open April to October (closed Mondays except Bank Holidays).

Acton Scott is not so much a museum as a working farm that lets in the public to watch. The imaginative aim was to re-create a farm of the late Victorian period before the appearance of the internal combustion engine. Its 22 acres (8.9 hectares) are stocked with cattle, sheep, pigs and poultry of the period, many of them now rare breeds, and routine farming operations are carried on throughout the year. There are static exhibits and demonstrations of country crafts throughout the season. Refreshments are available from the Schoolhouse Café. Local crafts and produce are on sale at the farm's two shops. Picnickers are welcome. Dogs are not allowed.

Bridgnorth

Bridgnorth Museum, Northgate, High Street, Bridgnorth. Telephone enquiries: 0746 762231.

Housed in the Burgess Hall of Northgate, above the traffic, the museum exhibits local history material, including many prints and paintings, a fine collection of fire-marks and an eighteenth-century turret clock.

Costume and Childhood Museum, Posterngate, Bridgnorth. Telephone: 0746 764636.

Open Mondays, Wednesdays to Saturdays and Sunday afternoons; closed on Tuesdays.

The museum features exhibits from the Victorian period onwards, including notable examples of costume and fashion, and bygones relating to tailoring, dressmaking and lace manufacture. There is also a display of early dolls and toys. Apart from the permanent collection, the museum stages temporary exhibitions on the theme of costume and fashion.

Longhorn cattle at the Acton Scott Historic Working Farm.

A BEA Viscount aircraft at the Aerospace Museum, Cosford.

Midland Motor Museum, Stanmore Hall, Stourbridge Road, Bridgnorth WV15 6DT. Telephone: 0746 761761.
Open weekends from March to October inclusive, and every day in July, August and September. Closed November to February inclusive.

This museum houses over one hundred vehicles — classic sports cars and sports and racing motorcycles mainly from the 1920s to 1980s, and a few early commercial and steam vehicles. Notable makes usually on display include Aston Martin, Bentley, Ferrari, Jaguar, Porsche, Rolls-Royce, AJS, BSA, MV, Norton, Triumph and Vincent. Many of the exhibits took part in competitive events when new, and some now take part in classic vehicle events. Also on display are collections of model cars and old petrol-pump globes.

Clun
Clun Local History Museum, Town Hall, Clun, Craven Arms. Telephone: 0588 640576.
Open Tuesday and Saturday afternoons from Easter to October; also the Saturday and Monday of Bank Holiday weekends.

This is a small museum run by the town itself. It is not continuously staffed but can usually be viewed on request. There is a display of domestic items but the main feature is a specialist collection of flints and geological items of local significance.

Cosford
Aerospace Museum, Cosford, Shifnal TF11 8UP. Telephone: 0902 374872. On the A41 Newport-Wolverhampton road, a short distance south of the M54 Junction 3.
Open daily except during the Christmas and New Year period.

This is one of the largest aircraft museums in Great Britain, although it started in a modest way in 1979 with a nucleus of surplus exhibits from the Royal Air Force Museum at Hendon, London. It houses the British Airways collection of civil aircraft, a magnificent array of Second World War planes from many of the combatant countries and some familiar post-war models like the Canberra, Meteor, Bristol 188 and the ill-fated TSR2. The collection of missiles, including the German V1 and V2, is probably the most comprehensive in the world. An acquisition of the 1980s is an Argentinian Pucara captured during the Falklands campaign of 1982. Apart from the aircraft themselves, there are associated exhibits and a shop for enthusiasts.

Llanymynech limestone quarries.

Ironbridge

Ironbridge Gorge Museum, Ironbridge, Telford TF8 7AW. Telephone: 0952 433522 (weekdays), 432166 (weekends). *Open daily.*

The Severn Gorge has a long history of industry. The availability within a small area of coal, iron ore, limestone and timber made it an early centre of ironmaking, and the river Severn was an ideal way of transporting raw materials and finished products. Before the eighteenth century, however, the iron was of too poor a quality for anything but small items such as ironmongery and cooking pots, and timber for charcoal burning was becoming scarce.

When Abraham Darby I moved to the area from Bristol in the early years of the eighteenth century he was already experimenting with alternative methods, and he finally perfected a means of smelting iron with coke rather than charcoal. The gorge, and in particular his works at nearby Coalbrookdale, became for a short time the technological centre of the world. He and his fellow ironmasters produced a series of pioneering achievements: the first iron rails, the first iron boat, the first iron-framed building. The monument to this innovation still stands. The world's first iron bridge, made by Abraham Darby III in 1779-81, spans the Severn by the little town named after it and is a good example of the huge castings made possible by the new techniques.

Ironbridge and Coalbrookdale made the industrial revolution possible, but when the Shropshire coalfield died and industry moved away the area was left as a wasteland with its achievements virtually forgotten. From the late nineteenth century onwards Ironbridge began to fossilise, and the relics of its industrial history were left for nature to reclaim.

During the 1960s two projects began to transform the district. One was the development of Telford New Town and the other was an ambitious scheme to create a complex of industrial museums. The new Museum Trust decided to concentrate renovation in certain areas while allowing Ironbridge and Coalbrookdale to retain as far as possible the appearance and atmosphere of industrial villages of the eighteenth and nineteenth centuries. Discreet restoration has been necessary, but tidying up has been kept to a minimum and prettifying has been avoided, so the visitor walking through Ironbridge today has no sense of being in a museum.

The museum sites are scattered over about 6 square miles (16 sq km). They include the following:

Blists Hill Open Air Museum, Legges Way, Madeley. This 42 acre (17 hectare) site is being developed as a living history of the working and social life of the gorge. Exhibits include two immense beam engines of the Lilleshall Company, reconstructed shops assembled in a street, Telford's tollhouse from Shelton near Shrewsbury, a tiny squatter's cottage with pigs and chickens, a carpenter's shop, a printing shop, a small coal mine, remains of blast furnaces, and the Hay Inclined Plane, which could lift boats from the Severn up to the Shropshire Canal in three and a half minutes.

Coalbrookdale Museum of Iron and Furnace, Coalbrookdale. This museum in a con-

The Coalport China Museum at Ironbridge.

verted warehouse covers objects made in iron and the whole field of ironmaking. The most remarkable exhibit outside is the original furnace of Abraham Darby I.

Coalport China Museum, Coalport. The Coalport Company moved its factory to Stoke-on-Trent in 1926, but the old works, including the kilns, now house displays explaining the processes of china making as well as an exhibition of some fine examples of decorative china produced here. There are regular demonstrations of pottery making.

Jackfield Tile Museum, Jackfield. On the south side of the river are the old Jackfield tileworks, where visitors can see the astonishing variety of floor and wall tiles turned out here since the late nineteenth century. Tile manufacture may be viewed and the Geology Gallery explains the background to the raw materials of the industrial revolution.

Museum of the River and Visitor Centre, The Wharfage, Ironbridge. Formerly the Severn Warehouse, where the Coalbrookdale iron

products were stored prior to shipment down the river, this museum includes a spectacular model of the gorge as it was in 1796.

Rosehill House, Coalbrookdale. Built in the early eighteenth century for a member of the Darby family, this house has been restored to illustrate the lifestyle of a Quaker ironmaster.

Other sites of interest include the **Tar Tunnel** at Coalport, from which natural tar was extracted; the **Bedlam Furnaces**; and the **Elton Gallery** at Coalbrookdale, containing pictures illustrating the development of industrial technology as well as changing exhibitions. The **Iron Bridge** itself is a public right of way for pedestrians, and the tollhouse nearby houses a small exhibition on the building of the bridge.

Ludlow

Buttercross Museum, Church Street, Ludlow. Telephone: 0584 873857. *Open April to end of September.*

The Buttercross is itself of great interest —

The Bedlam Furnaces at Ironbridge.

an eighteenth-century building in ornate style once used as a school. There is a display of local history, providing a chronological story of Ludlow from prehistoric to Victorian times. A visit before touring the town is recommended.

Much Wenlock

Much Wenlock Museum, High Street, Much Wenlock TF13 6HR. Telephone: 0952 727773.

Open April to end of September.

This is a museum of local history and geography run by the County Museum Service. Many of the exhibits are related to trades that once flourished in the town, such as wheelwrighting, leathercraft and brewing, but there are also bygones of domestic life, displays on the geology and natural history of Wenlock Edge, and a special feature on the Wenlock Olympian Society, whose founder, Dr William Brookes, played a part in establishing the modern Olympic Games.

Onibury

The Wernlas Collection, Shropshire's Rare Breeds Centre, Green Lane, Onibury, Craven Arms SY7 9BL. Telephone: 058477 318. 4 miles (6 km) north-west of Ludlow off the A49.

Open daily, except Mondays (but open on Bank Holidays).

The Wernlas Collection is the United Kingdom's leading conservation centre for rare and minority breeds of large fowl. These colourful and fascinating birds are displayed in a spectacular setting along with other rare breeds of farm animals.

Oswestry

Oswestry Heritage and Exhibition Centre, The Old Grammar School, Church Street, Oswestry SY11 2TE. Telephone: 0691 671323.

Open Mondays to Saturdays throughout the year, and Sundays in summer.

In this picturesque timber-framed house in the town's churchyard, built in 1407 as a free grammar school, exhibits illustrating local life and history are displayed and occasional exhibitions are staged. There are a café and a shop.

Oswestry Transport Museum, Oswald Road, Oswestry. Telephone: 0691 671749. *Open daily.*

Oswestry was the headquarters of the former Cambrian Railway, and one of the old engine sheds now houses an extensive collection of railway memorabilia and artefacts. Locomotives and rolling stock are also on view, occasionally in steam. There is also a fine collection of old bicycles and cycling bygones.

Park Hall Working Farm Museum, Park Hall, Whittington, Oswestry SY11 4AS. Telephone: 0691 652175.

Open May to October, daily except Fridays, but open on Fridays too in July, August and the first two weeks of September.

This is a Victorian farm displaying working practices of the last 120 years and also a notable centre for the breeding of Shire horses.

Shrewsbury

Clive House Museum, College Hill, Shrewsbury SY1 1LT. Telephone: 0743 354811.

Open weekdays all year.

This elegant eighteenth-century house was associated with Robert Clive (Clive of India), when he was Mayor of Shrewsbury in 1762. There are displays of Shropshire porcelains (Caughley and Coalport). Period rooms, a Victorian kitchen and toy room evoke the social and domestic life of Shrewsbury in the eighteenth and nineteenth centuries.

Rowley's House Museum, Barker Street, Shrewsbury SY1 1QH. Telephone: 0743 361196.

Open weekdays all year, Sundays Easter to end of September.

The museum occupies two buildings of great historical interest. The timber-framed sixteenth-century warehouse is one of the town's showpieces, and the adjoining seventeenth-century brick mansion has now been incorporated to form extensive premises. There are costume, geology, prehistory, natural and local history galleries, with major displays relating to the excavation of the nearby Roman city of *Viroconium* (see page 49). There are some remarkable artefacts, including a silver mirror and the carved inscription from the front of the forum.

Shrewsbury Castle is the home of the Shropshire Regimental Museum.

Shropshire Regimental Museum, The Castle, Shrewsbury SY1 2AT. Telephone: 0743 358516.
Temporarily closed following a terrorist bombing in 1992.
The collections of the King's Shropshire Light Infantry, the Shropshire Yeomanry Cavalry and the Shropshire Royal Horse Artillery are housed in Shrewsbury Castle, which dates from 1083 and last saw service during the Civil War. In 1992 a terrorist bomb destroyed many of the displays and the museum is closed for renovation and conservation.

Telford
(See also under Ironbridge)
Hoo Farm Country Park, Preston upon the Weald Moors, Telford TF6 6DJ. Telephone: 0952 677917.
Open Easter to September and end of November to Christmas.

This farm with a difference features all sorts of unusual farming activities and animals, including ostriches, tame llamas and deer and steeplechasing sheep. There are a farm trail, a shop and a tea room.

Underwater World, Buildwas Road, Dale End Park, Ironbridge TF8 7DW. Telephone: 0952 432484.
Open weekday afternoons, and mornings also at weekends and Bank Holidays and in school holidays.
This is a unique opportunity to see at close quarters the wide variety of fish to be found in the river Severn.

Wroxeter
Viroconium Museum, Wroxeter Roman City, Wroxeter, Shrewsbury SY5 6PH. See page 49.

9
Industrial history

Shropshire has a distinguished history of industrial enterprise. The remains of coalfields, ironworks, lead mines, quarries, railways, canals and potteries can all be found, many of them in the process of preservation by the Ironbridge Gorge Museum Trust (see page 81). Other relics are simply there for the enterprising visitor to seek out. The enthusiast will probably want to consult a gazetteer (the best is the West Midland volume of Fred Brook's *Industrial Archaeology of the British Isles*) but the following sites are likely to be of interest to the non-specialist.

Castle Hill Cliff Railway, Bridgnorth
   The Cliff Railway is not a relic: it was opened in 1892 and is still working, running a frequent service between High Town and the riverside. Operated now by electricity, the cars were originally propelled up and down by running water in and out of tanks beneath them. The slope is fearsome.

Coleham Pumping Station, Longden Coleham, Shrewsbury. Telephone: 0743 361196. *Open by appointment only.*
   Until 1970 Shrewsbury relied on Victorian pumping engines for its sewage operations. The superb Renshaw engines have been preserved at Coleham.

Daniels Mill, Eardington, Bridgnorth WV16 5JL. Telephone: 0746 762753. *Open weekends and Bank Holiday Mondays from Easter to end of September (afternoons only from Easter to end of May).*
   Daniels Mill is a working watermill with a spectacular wheel, producing stoneground wholemeal flour for sale. There are also an exhibition of bygones and a gift shop, and light refreshments are available.

Ironbridge and Coalbrookdale
   The sites of historical interest have now been taken over by the Ironbridge Gorge Museum Trust (page 81) but a walk through these two communities enables one to absorb their atmosphere and to study the houses and public buildings, which remain virtually unaltered. Good walking guides to Coalbrookdale and Coalport are available at the museum bookstalls.

Llanymynech
   There are spectacular limestone workings here (OS 126: SJ 264217). Walk out of the

One of the cars on the Castle Hill Cliff Railway at Bridgnorth.

Thomas Telford's aqueduct at Longdon-on-Tern, the first to be built in cast iron.

village on the Oswestry road for a few hundred yards and take the narrow path that runs beside the first of the council houses on the left. It takes you to the top of a tramway incline, where there are substantial remains of a winding house. The path to the left of this leads to the main workings, including a huge tunnel. It is possible to trace the routes of the limestone down to the Montgomeryshire Canal, where the former processing site has now been turned into a heritage area. It contains old bottle kilns and a vast Hoffman rotary kiln, as well as the canal docks from which the lime was shipped.

Longdon-on-Tern (OS 127: SJ 617156)

This was Telford's first attempt, in 1795, to construct a cast-iron canal aqueduct. It has been preserved, although the Shrewsbury Canal, which it was built to carry, disappeared long ago. Telford used this structure as a prototype for his celebrated Pontcysyllte Aqueduct near Llangollen.

Market Drayton

There is an interesting canal depot just outside the town (OS 127: SJ 684347). It is busy in summer with holiday craft, and part of the complex has been turned into a marina.

Montgomeryshire Canal

The Shropshire section of what is now called the Montgomeryshire Canal (but was historically the Ellesmere Canal) ran from a junction with what is now the Llangollen Canal at Welsh Frankton (OS 126: SJ 371318) to Llanymynech on the Welsh border. It was part of the Shropshire Union system when it became unnavigable following a breach in 1936. Built at the end of the eighteenth century, its purpose was to carry away the limestone from the Llanymynech quarries, although extensions were later carried through to Newtown. About half the Shropshire section is now dry, but there are plans to restore full navigation.

Sites of particular interest are:

Welsh Frankton locks. The four locks lower the canal 30 feet (9 metres). This was once an important place with a canal tavern (the white house on the west bank) and a boatbuilder's workshop and dry dock situated beside the bottom lock.

Lockgate Bridge (OS 126: SJ 368310). Here can be seen a projected branch to Shrewsbury that was never completed (see Westonwharf, page 88). The incomplete length was used occasionally and closed in 1917.

Rednal rail/canal interchange (OS 126: SJ 352279). A cut from the canal leads to a large basin, which connected with sidings from the Shrewsbury-Chester railway line above. The interchange was abandoned in the 1850s.

Rednal passenger interchange (OS 126: SJ 351276). A short-lived scheme in the 1850s provided for fast passenger boats from Newtown to connect with the railway at Rednal and West Felton station nearby. The square brick and timber building close to the railway bridge is believed to have been the passenger terminal. Next to it is one of the very few 'roving bridges' on the canal, designed to let the horse cross to the opposite towpath without unhitching the towrope.

Queen's Head (OS 126: SJ 339268). The corn mill that received supplies of wheat by canal from Ellesmere Port still stands. In the centre of the green corrugated iron shed beside the canal is a low tunnel used for donkey-hauled wagons from the sandpits in the fields behind.

Maesbury Marsh (OS 126: SJ 314250). This is a rare example of a canal village. It has a warehouse, canal tavern (still in business), a restored wharf with crane and stabling at the back of the inn.

Pant (OS 126: SJ 277224). This was once a busy waterfront, loading limestone from the quarries above. In the centre of the village a path leads away from the main road at SJ 274219 to reach a restored winding drum at the top of an incline. The minor road a few yards to the west leads to the bottom of the incline, where there is a wharf with limekilns.

Oswestry

The town was once the headquarters of the Cambrian Railways, and the former station area is of interest. The imposing station building still stands, converted to a shop and flats. Next to it is the yard of the Cambrian Railways Society, a preservation group, and the buildings housing the Oswestry Transport Museum (see page 83). To the north are the extensive buildings that used to house the engineering workshops, with the long footbridge that gave access to them across the tracks. The railway station at Gobowen is famous for its Italianate architecture.

Severn Valley Railway. At Bridgnorth railway station, close to the town centre. Administrative offices at The Railway Station, Bewdley, Worcestershire DY12 1BG. Telephone: 0299 403816.

Trains run at weekends from mid March to the New Year holiday, and every day from mid May to the end of September.

The Severn Valley Railway is one of the longest restored standard-gauge railways in Britain, running over 16 miles (26 km) of track between Bridgnorth and Kidderminster. It has developed remarkably since its foundation in 1965 and is now a major commercial enterprise whose shares are much sought after. However, it still relies largely on a nucleus of enthusiastic volunteers to maintain and run a very professional operation.

Welsh Frankton locks.

From the northern terminus at Bridgnorth the line follows the river Severn closely through attractive countryside, with intermediate stations at Eardington, Hampton Loade, Highley, Arley, Northwood, and Bewdley. The railway operates from the beginning of March to the end of November with a varying frequency of trains. At weekends in July and August there can be as many as ten trips per day each way, but before planning a visit it is advisable to check the timetable, available at all local information centres.

In addition to steam-hauled train travel, there is a good deal to see. At Bridgnorth are the locomotive sheds and workshops while Bewdley houses the carriage and wagon works and has an interesting model railway layout. A new station in traditional style was built for the SVR at Kidderminster, opened in 1984, as the line's southern terminus.

Shrewsbury

On the north side of the railway station in Howard Street is the former canal terminus, with a very elegant warehouse of 1835. A short distance further north in Spring Gardens is a large malting, originally a flax mill built in 1796-7 and reputed to be the world's first iron-framed building; the sections were cast at William Hazledine's foundry in Shrewsbury.

Snailbeach

This former lead-mining district is reached by taking the A488 from Shrewsbury and turning on to a minor road $1^1/_2$ miles (2.4 km) after Minsterley. Mining began here in Roman times and reached a peak in the late nineteenth century, when Snailbeach had the most productive mine in Europe. Although nature is rapidly reclaiming the sites (and also many of the smallholdings carved out by miners) many relics can still be discovered. The approach to the area is marked by heaps of white spoil, and a lane beside them (signposted Lordshill) provides a parking space. There is an old engine house here, and the main workings are reached by walking a few hundred yards further up the hill. The former Bog Mine area can be visited (see page 38).

Telford

In Hadley Park, Leegomery, a guillotine-type lock of the Shrewsbury Canal has been preserved, the only one with complete mechanism. The Stirchley Chimney in the Town Park is all that remains of a group of furnaces that used to occupy the site in the nineteenth century.

Telford Steam Railway, Bridge Road, Horsehay, Telford TF4 2NF. Telephone: 0952 503880. Off the A5223 or B4373 at Horsehay.
Open at weekends. Trains run the last Sunday in the month and Bank Holidays from Easter to the end of September; tram runs every Sunday in the same period.

The Trust preserves six steam locomotives and a variety of rolling stock near the site of a former station and depot that once served many pits and ironworks. The tramway between Coalbrookdale and Horsehay is believed to have been the first to be fitted with iron rails in 1767, and the former Horsehay Ironworks was established nearby by Abraham Darby in 1755. The Horsehay Pool, which still survives, was connected with the ironworks. The Trust operates Britain's only narrow-gauge steam tram.

Titterstone Clee

There are extensive remains of quarry buildings on the top of the hill (OS 137:SO 593775) and the long inclines that carried roadstone to the bottom can be walked.

Westonwharf

The final link in the Ellesmere Canal Company's scheme to join the Severn and the Mersey with a trunk waterway was to have been a canal from Welsh Frankton to Shrewsbury. It was never completed, and the arm came to an end in the middle of fields at Westonwharf (OS 126:SJ 420256). It was nevertheless used until 1917, and at the bottom end of the hamlet the dried-up wharf with limekilns and warehouse can still be seen. They are on private property but can be viewed from the road.

10
Shropshire people

Most of the people included in this chapter are undoubtedly famous, while a few ought to be but have somehow escaped the public attention their achievements deserve. Some were born in the county; others have been adopted with pride.

Agnes Hunt was born in 1870 at Boreatton Park, Baschurch. At the age of nine she contracted osteomyelitis, but this crippling condition did not prevent her from qualifying as a nurse after rigorous training. Soon afterwards her mother persuaded her to open a convalescent home for children in a house on the Boreatton estate, run on the theory that the best restoratives were plentiful food and un-limited fresh air. Her patients were installed in wooden sheds in the garden with one side open to the elements, and she persuaded the orthopaedic surgeon Robert Jones to visit the home regularly and even carry out operations on her dining room table.

Against all the odds Agnes Hunt's 'hospital' flourished and attracted such wide support that in 1921 she was able to found a new establishment in the old military hospital at Park Hall, Oswestry. It was more orthodox but run on the same principles, and Robert Jones again gave his assistance. Six years later she established the Derwen Training College for disabled people on a nearby site. After a fire in 1948 the present Robert Jones and Agnes Hunt Orthopaedic Hospital was built. It has since become internationally recognised for innovative work, while the Derwen College continues to flourish. Agnes Hunt died in 1948 and her ashes are buried in the churchyard at Baschurch. There is a memorial plaque in the church itself.

When Agnes Hunt was six years old another girl was born only a few miles away who was destined to have even greater success in breaking away from the traditional role of rural middle-class women. **Eglantyne Jebb** was born at The Lyth, Ellesmere, and went to Oxford University, where she decided to pursue a career of social service. Having failed to become a successful primary school teacher, she began to take an interest in the problem of Balkan refugees, making a hazardous journey to the area. After the First World War, when the number of refugees had grown alarmingly, she started a campaign to rescue European children from starvation and in 1919 organised a mass meeting at the Albert Hall to launch what was imaginatively called the 'Save the Children Fund'. Although she was criticised for refusing to make British children her first priority, she was determined that the Fund should be international, and she showed remarkable political adroitness to achieve her aim. She was only 52 when she died and is buried at Geneva, an appropriate place for one who inaugurated what has become one of the largest international charities.

At Plas Wilmot in Oswestry the poet **Wilfred Owen** was born in 1893, the son of a railway worker. The man who might have become the leading poet of his generation survived some of the worst fighting of the First World War only to be killed by a stray bullet a week before the Armistice, at the age of 25. A house where Owen lived, in Monkmoor Road, Shrewsbury, is marked by a plaque, and his favourite walk to Uffington can still be followed. Owen spent only a few years of his early life in Oswestry, but **Henry Walford Davies** had deeper roots since his family had been established in the town for many years and had close associations with the Congregational church and local choirs. Davies received a sound musical training and was appointed in 1898 to the prestigious post of organist at the Temple Church in London. Encouraged by Elgar, he started serious composition, producing his popular *Solemn Melody* in 1908. In 1934 he succeeded Elgar as Master of the King's Musick and until his death in 1941 had a dual career as an academic and populariser of music through radio broadcasts.

Oswestry's most distinguished daughter was the novelist **Barbara Pym**, who has become recognised in recent years as one of Britain's finest modern writers of comedy. She spent the first twenty years of her life at Morda Lodge in Morda Road.

Whittington, just to the east of Oswestry, claims to have produced Dick Whittington, but while this claim lacks substance the village can point to two local celebrities of widely contrasting characters. The solid Victorian interior of the church was created as a memorial to its most distinguished incumbent, **William Walsam How**. He was rector here for 28 years and went on to become a notable bishop, but he is best remembered as a hymn writer. **'Mad Jack' Mytton** was born in 1796 at Halston Hall just outside Whittington. His wild exploits have passed into local legend, and further afield he has come to typify the hard-drinking, hard-riding country squire of the Regency period, running rapidly through the family money and ending his life in a debtors' prison at the age of 38.

Charles Darwin's statue in Shrewsbury.

Whitchurch, like Oswestry, produced a composer of great popular appeal. **Edward German** was born in St Mary's Lane in 1862 and became a well-known composer of operetta and incidental music for the theatre. He worked with Gilbert and Sullivan on two Savoy operas, but his most enduring work has been his *Merrie England* published in 1902.

Whitchurch has its poet too. **George Turberville** was born there in about 1540, and although his name may not be familiar he has a distinguished place in English literary history as one of the earliest experimenters with blank verse, the form that Shakespeare was later to perfect.

Wem can claim the essayist **William Hazlitt**, who lived in Noble Street in his youth; **John Ireland**, who wrote a famous biography of the artist Hogarth; and **William Betty**, who retired here after a career on the London stage. Betty, known as the Young Roscius, was a child prodigy who so fascinated audiences in the late eighteenth century that on one occasion the proceedings of the House of Commons were suspended so that MPs could attend one of his performances.

William Wycherley, one of the outstanding dramatists of the Restoration period, was born in the village of Clive, north of Shrewsbury, in 1640. He had an erratic career, being bought out of a debtors' prison by James II, but his best plays, *The Country Wife* and *The Plain Dealer*, are still performed today. One of Wycherley's schoolmates at Shrewsbury was **George Jeffreys**, the notorious judge of the 'Bloody Assize' that followed the Duke of Monmouth's rebellion in the West Country. He was born near Wrexham, but after being appointed Lord Chief Justice at the age of 38 he bought the manors of Loppington and Wem from Wycherley and became Baron Jeffreys of Wem, with his official residence at Lowe Hall just outside the town.

Another famous figure from this period was **Admiral Benbow**. His father was a Shrewsbury tanner, and his uncle is remembered as the man who guided the Parliamentary forces through Shrewsbury's Royalist defences by way of the water gate near the castle. John Benbow joined the navy in 1677 at the age of 24 and quickly obtained a command of his own. He distinguished himself in the kind of short and bloody engagements that appeal to the public, and after dying of wounds in Jamaica in 1702 he became the subject of countless inn signs. His official memorial is in St Mary's, Shrewsbury.

Shrewsbury's most famous citizen has a more public monument. A statue of **Charles Darwin** stands opposite the castle entrance in front of what was once his school and is now the public library. His birthplace, a large house in Frankwell called The Mount, is now used as offices. His time at Shrewsbury School seems to have been marked by passive rebellion against the non-scientific curriculum, and his interest in natural history found no outlet in his medical studies at Edinburgh or in his later theological training. It was at Edinburgh, however, that he began to study the new science of geology and started to question the biblical account of the Creation.

The turning point in Darwin's life came in 1831, when he was invited to join a Royal Navy surveying expedition to the Pacific. He was only 22, but his prolific and scrupulous observations of natural history gained him an immediate scientific reputation. The expedition also provided the first evidence for his momentous theory of evolution, which he had completed by 1843 but did not publish until 1859. *The Origin of Species* and *The Descent of Man* caused an intellectual uproar that has not entirely subsided. By 1882, however, the controversy had quietened sufficiently to allow Darwin to be buried in Westminster Abbey.

Shrewsbury Abbey has become well known through the novels of **Ellis Peters** (Edith Pargeter), who lives in Shropshire. This and other places associated with her fictional monk-detective Brother Cadfael have become the basis for 'tourist trails' in the county.

The eastern outskirts of Shrewsbury are dominated by a lofty column standing outside the modern Shire Hall. It commemorates **Rowland Hill**, who would have achieved far greater fame as a soldier if his immediate superior had not been the first Duke of Wellington. He served throughout the Peninsular War and the Battle of Waterloo as Wellington's leading general, and his promotion to Commander-in-Chief in 1828 marked the beginning of a period in which the army had

very little to do. He was probably Shropshire's outstanding soldier, although he could not match the talents of **Sir Philip Sidney**, another former pupil of Shrewsbury School. As soldier, poet, scholar and courtier Sidney was regarded in the Elizabethan age as the ideal of the Renaissance man. His death at the battle of Zutphen, where he was fighting for the Dutch against the Spanish, is happily commemorated by the fact that Zutphen is Shrewsbury's twin town.

The patriarchal **Abraham Darby I** came to the Severn Gorge from Bristol in 1690, but successive generations of Salopian Darbys dominated Ironbridge and Coalbrookdale until the twentieth century. The leading figure on the other side of the river was **John Wilkinson** of Broseley, who first proved that iron boats would float and later designed his own iron coffin.

Despite the impact made on the area by these industrialists, when it came to naming the new town to be built on the old Shropshire coalfield it was a Scot, **Thomas Telford**, who was honoured. This was appropriate because although Telford's work extended throughout Britain and Europe it was in Shropshire that he made his name. He was born in Eskdale in southern Scotland in 1757 and had already done major work as a stonemason when he arrived in Shrewsbury in 1786. He had been recommended to Sir William Pulteney, MP for Shrewsbury, who was looking for someone to convert the decaying castle into a house. Afterwards Pulteney's influence secured Telford the post of County Surveyor. He soon revealed himself as a master of many trades, supervising the construction of Shrewsbury prison and infirmary, building churches at Bridgnorth and Madeley, constructing several dozen bridges, designing the first cast-iron aqueduct at Longdon-on-Tern, advising on the Ellesmere and Shrewsbury canals and remaking the Shropshire section of the Holyhead Road. He approached the last task with characteristic thoroughness, designing the milestones (many of them are still in position) and the tollhouses. One of these, from Shelton, Shrewsbury, is now at the Blists Hill Open Air Museum, Ironbridge; another still stands on the eastern outskirts of Oswestry, while a third, of a somewhat differ-

Thomas Telford.

1760 he became MP for Shrewsbury, living at Clive House, now a museum. The end of his life was overshadowed by ill health, both physical and mental, and by a long campaign against him in Parliament. The exact cause of his death is not clear, but he is buried in an obscure grave at Moreton Say and commemorated only by a simple wall memorial in the church.

On the road between Shrewsbury and Ludlow is the village of Bromfield, birthplace in 1800 of **Henry Hickman**, an early advocate of anaesthesia. He spent much of his short life trying to persuade medical authorities in England and France to take his ideas seriously but died in 1830 with no credit for his work. He was buried in Bromfield churchyard, but it was not until 1930 that the Royal College of Surgeons placed a memorial plaque in the church.

Ludlow was the home of **Stanley Weyman**, whose novels of exotic adventure like *Under the Red Robe* were immensely popular at the beginning of the twentieth century. **Samuel Butler** lived here for a time also, but the town is associated most strongly with **A. E. Housman**. Housman was born in Worcestershire and had few connections with Shropshire; he admitted that the county was simply a remote and romantic setting for a collections of poems of 1896 to which he gave the title *A Shropshire Lad* as an afterthought. Yet in a strange way he managed to encapsulate much of what the county means to those who live in it, and it is appropriate that his ashes should have been buried in Ludlow churchyard.

One town that Housman did know well was Much Wenlock. In 1850 a local doctor, **William Brookes**, founded the Wenlock Olympians, one of the earliest British athletics clubs, and then went on to play a major part with Baron de Coubertin in reviving the Olympic Games. He is commemorated in the church and the local secondary school is named after him. Further down the Bridgnorth road is the village of Morville, where the 'big house' is Aldenham Hall. It is the home of the **Actons**, one of Shropshire's oldest and most distinguished families, whose members have often found exotic niches in history. Sir John Acton became prime mini-

ent pattern, can be seen at Montford Bridge.

One of the constituent areas of Telford New Town is Dawley, once a town in its own right and the birthplace of **Captain Matthew Webb**, the pioneer marathon swimmer. He completed the first Channel swim in 1875 and performed some remarkable feats after that, but he did not survive his attempt to swim across the bottom of Niagara Falls in 1883.

The most famous native of the county's eastern border was **Robert Clive**, born at Moreton Say near Market Drayton in 1725. The man who played a major part in securing India for the British Empire was a lawless youth, and in India he showed the same disregard for convention and regulations, pursuing single-mindedly the interests of British trade and his own financial advantage. In

ster of Naples at the end of the eighteenth century, while a little later Charles Acton rose to be a cardinal with considerable influence in the Vatican. The first Lord Acton was a famous nineteenth-century historian, whose *Lectures in Modern History* became a classic.

At Bridgnorth, one of the showpieces is Bishop Percy's House in Cartway. **Thomas Percy** was born in 1729, the son of a grocer apparently called Pearcy (Thomas spent much time in trying to establish a link with the Percy family of Northumberland). He was educated at the local grammar school and was ordained as a minister of the church. While on a visit to a friend's house in Shifnal he noticed a housemaid lighting a fire with pages from an old book, which he rescued. It contained some early English ballads, and Percy became so interested that he induced his friends to search libraries for similar examples, publishing the collection as *Reliques of Ancient English Poetry* in 1765. It produced a sensation in literary circles and strongly influenced the new generation of romantic poets who were rebelling against the formal classical verse of the eighteenth century. Percy eventually became Bishop of Dromore in Ireland.

A less illustrious but better known Bridgnorth figure was **Francis Moore**. In 1701 he published the first of a series of annual prognostications later to become famous as Old Moore's Almanac.

Close by St Leonard's church in Bridgnorth is the cottage that **Richard Baxter**, the saintly Puritan preacher, occupied in 1640-1. He was born at Eaton Constantine and went to school at Wroxeter. Trained as an orthodox Anglican priest, he served a memorable ministry at Kidderminster, but in later life he turned towards nonconformity and found himself increasingly at odds with the ethos of the Restoration, both in church and state. His conscience impelled him to speak out and he was imprisoned as a dissenter by Judge Jeffreys.

At Cleobury Mortimer, on the southern border of Shropshire, the east window of the parish church commemorates **William Langland**, the contemporary of Chaucer who was born there in about 1330 and is best remembered for his satire *The Vision of Piers Plowman*.

The writer whose work was most strongly influenced by the county was **Mary Webb**. She was born Gladys Meredith in 1891 at Leighton, a small village near Ironbridge. Her father moved house fairly frequently and the family lived at The Grange, Much Wenlock, Harcourt Manor at Stanton upon Hine Heath, and at Meole Brace, now a suburb of Shrewsbury. It was at Meole Brace church in 1912 that she married Henry Webb, a schoolmaster. After two years as a teacher's wife in Weston-super-Mare she persuaded her husband to move to a house in Pontesbury, where she settled to serious writing. The couple lived partly off the produce of their large garden, which Mary sold from a stall in Shrewsbury market. Her final home was at Lyth Hill, south of Shrewsbury.

Mary Webb's critical reputation has waxed and waned over the years. All her books are dominated by the Shropshire landscape, and as a regional novelist she probably ranks after Thomas Hardy. Modern readers, however, find it difficult to accept the melodramatic atmosphere of her work, which gains its effect by contrasting youth and innocence with menacing and primitive rustic passions. It is a compliment to her (but perhaps her misfortune) that she inspired Stella Gibbons to write *Cold Comfort Farm*, a parody that became much more popular than its original. After a lifetime of poor health Mary Webb died in 1927.

11
Tourist information centres

Those marked with an asterisk (*) are open in the summer only. Those marked with an obelus (†) are tourist information points with limited facilities (no accommodation booking service).

Bishop's Castle†: Old Time, 29 High Street, Bishop's Castle. Telephone: 0538 638437.
Bridgnorth: The Library, Listley Street, Bridgnorth WV16 4AW. Telephone: 0746 763358.
Church Stretton*: The Library, Church Street, Church Stretton SY6 6DQ. Telephone: 0694 723133.
Ellesmere†: Visitor Centre, The Mere, Ellesmere. Telephone: 0691 622981.
Ironbridge: The Wharfage, Ironbridge, Telford TF8 7AW. Telephone: 0952 432166.
Ludlow: Castle Street, Ludlow SY8 1AS. Telephone: 0584 875053.
Market Drayton†: The Clive Library, 51 Cheshire Street, Market Drayton. Telephone: 0630 652139.
Much Wenlock*: Guildhall, Barrow Street, Much Wenlock TF13 6AE. Telephone: 0952 727679.
Newport: 76/78 High Street, Newport TF10 7AU. Telephone: 0952 814109.
Oswestry: Mile End Service Area, A5, Oswestry SY11 4JA. Telephone: 0691 662488.
Shrewsbury: The Music Hall, The Square, Shrewsbury SY1 1LH. Telephone: 0743 350761.
Telford: Shopping Centre, Telford TF3 4BX. Telephone: 0952 291370.
Wellington: Tan Bank, 1 Landau Court, Wellington, Telford TF1 1BD. Telephone: 0952 48295.
Whitchurch: The Civic Centre, High Street, Whitchurch SY13 1AX. Telephone: 0948 4577.

12
Further reading

Edwards, J. F. *Walks for Motorists: Shropshire and the North Wales Border*. Frederick Warne, 1991.
Garner, Lawrence. *The Buildings of Shropshire: Tudor and Stuart*. Swan Hill Press, 1989.
Garner, Lawrence. *The Buildings of Shropshire: Georgian and Regency*. Swan Hill Press, 1980.
Jackson, Michael. *Castles of Shropshire*. Shropshire Books, 1988.
Morriss, R. K. *Railways of Shropshire*. Shropshire Books, revised 1991.
Morriss, R. K. *Canals of Shropshire*. Shropshire Books, 1992.
Pevsner, Nikolaus. *The Buildings of England: Shropshire*. Penguin, 1958.
Rowley, Trevor. *The Shropshire Landscape*. Hodder and Stoughton, 1972.
Stanford, S. C. *The Archaeology of the Welsh Marches*. Collins, 1980; revised edition published by the author, 1991.
Toghill, Peter. *Geology in Shropshire*. Swan Hill Press, 1990.
Trinder, Barrie. *The Industrial Revolution in Shropshire*. Phillimore, 1973.
Waite, Vincent. *Shropshire Hill Country*. Phillimore, 1981.

FICTION
The novelist Mary Webb evokes the Shropshire landscape in fiercely romantic fashion, particularly in *The Golden Arrow* (1916), *Precious Bane* (1925) and *Gone to Earth* (1933). The 'Brother Cadfael' detective novels of Ellis Peters vividly portray Shrewsbury and the surrounding countryside in the twelfth century.

Index

Page numbers in italics refer to illustrations.